Rising to the Call

This book is dedicated to our fellow seekers—
peers and students, teachers all.

A HANDBOOK FOR EVOLVING SOULS

Rising to the Call

Healing Ourselves and Helping Others in the Coming Era

Jacquelyn Small
and
Mary Yovino

DeVorss & Company, Publishers

ISBN: 0-87516-704-7
Library of Congress Catalog Card No.: 96-72566

DeVorss & Co.
P.O. Box 550
Marina del Rey, CA 90294

Printed in the United States of America

Table of Contents

Table of Exercises

From the Authors . . . .

Why We Wrote This Book

Rising to the Call was designed for these troubled times. Between us—though not in equal shares—we have almost 30 years of active, on-site experience observing and guiding people who struggle with the very common problems of simply being human, as we've been doing ourselves. Whether it be "not fitting in," feeling "less than," dealing with specific clinical issues, or even being "high" on some form of inspiration, all our fellow travelers reflect what's going on in the world today, while searching for meaning in the human struggle.

A consensus among modern thinkers in many different disciplines, including science, art, and philosophy, sees spiritual awakening as *the only hope for survival* of this planet and its inhabitants. And so we present a basic *spiritual psychology* to support the massive survival effort that's so badly needed.

This is about people choosing to heal and move on into new ways of being, no longer ruled by the past, which is a prerequisite to—and goes hand-in-hand with—helping others to do the same. We've written this book for those who are willing to stand up for all they truly are, consciously deciding to accelerate their processes of growth, even though it sometimes hurts.

This book is for all who are interested in a powerful all-encompassing psychological health and spiritual awakening, whether their own or that of people they serve. This material is relevant for all evolving souls, whether or not they work in the "people-helping" professions. We believe you will find the language to be down-to-earth; and we give practical examples, so you can easily apply the principles to everyday life. For everyone is called to help others from time to time, regardless of their official roles.

Periodically, a meditative exercise will give you the opportunity to interrupt your reading for some contemplation or experiential inner work. We suggest you pause to do these exercises as you come to them, take them in, and allow this to become a *living* process. Later you might want to tape the exercises for ongoing use in your personal or professional practice. And if you do plan to use them with others, be sure to try them yourself first.

Some Primary Themes

The information we've compiled here is the backbone of our work, which unfolds around such themes as:

- Evolution
- Psyche and Soul
- Creative Imagination and Co-creating the Future
- The Shadow
- Service

Simply stated, **evolution** puts the far-reaching current world crises into a positive light by teaching that what's happening today was *meant* to happen; and that we have every reason to believe what's ahead will be an advancement toward the spiritual unfolding of humankind.

From our work with hundreds of seekers, we've developed a reverent respect for the human **psyche**, that wise inner Being of enormous proportions and spiritual stature who functions in the mind. Throughout these pages you will find key reminders, over and over, of how to be ''in this world and not of it''—to live it all completely, and to absorb the conditions here from the standpoint of the **soul's** sacred activities.

We talk about the **creative imagination** in terms of psyche and ''the new physics,'' as they both relate to humankind's capacity and responsibility for **''co-creating'' the future**. You'll see how very much you have to do with establishing the meaning in your life, continuously designing your own reality. And you'll learn to do so consciously by awakening the forgotten soul power of imaginative cognition. For you simply can never have what you cannot imagine!

The **''shadow,''** which has a dark, lurking connotation in whatever context it's used, is an entity we've come to wholly appreciate (even though it isn't always welcome). Again we'll share what we've learned from observation and personal experience—how anyone can learn to honor his or her individual shadow, or ''dark side,'' how cultivating a healthy relationship with your personal shadow heals your psyche.

And we present the concept of **service** from an uplifting perspective too. Quite different from the idealistic view of service as totally selfless, where the needs of others must always take precedence over one's own, we use a broader interpretation. Quoting the Tibetan Djwhal Khul:

> "True service is the spontaneous outflow of a loving heart and an intelligent mind; it is the result of being in the right place and staying there; it is produced by the inevitable inflow of spiritual force and not by strenuous physical plane activity; it is the effect of a man's being what he truly is, a divine Son of God, and not by the studied effect of his words or deeds."
>
> —*A Treatise on White Magic*

Significant Elements

Two of the most important topics in this book are covered in sections called:

- *Our Many Selves,* and
- *Characteristics of Effective Healers.*

In "Our Many Selves," we discuss those elusive parts within human nature that are so key to evolution, but often are misunderstood or even go completely unrecognized. Besides describing the sacred functions of these "inner beings" as they help in human evolution, we outline simple procedures for befriending each of them; and show how recognition of these selves enhances their productivity.

In Part 3, "Characteristics of Effective Healers" explains ten traits that research has shown to be common among professional helpers who "get results" with their clients. In other words, when people make use of certain characteristics in their dealings with others—*whether or not* it's in an actual counseling situation—everyone gains from the relationship.

In this section, typical dialogs illustrate how each trait works in its own healing way. We also point out how hurtful—even toxic—human interactions can be when, instead of being used properly, the *opposite* of the healing trait is played out.

A Word about Definitions

Several parts of *Rising to the Call* are dedicated to redefining certain familiar psychological concepts. They give new perspectives, and compare the new with older definitions that are now becoming outmoded.

Besides those specific sections, other terms scattered throughout the book are highlighted to point out that they too are being used in a context fitting for the 1990's and on into the next cycle. You'll recognize this by the **TERM** being shown in boldface. Then a definitive discussion will give its meaning as it applies to this book.

Inviting Your Thoughts

Since our work is highly interactive, gaining substance from real-life conditions, we welcome feedback from readers.

Either of us can be reached through Eupsychia, the company whose address and telephone numbers are provided on page 218. And we would love to meet you face to face some-time at a workshop or seminar!

But whether or not we ever hear from you directly, you are in our hearts. As you read along, we hope you can actually feel—as we do—the sense of soulful mystery this current dimensional shift carries with it. And we wish you well as you enter into a life more expressive of your soul's ideals.

—JS and MY

What Is This Call We Hear?

"What is it, in the end, that induces a man to go his own way, and to rise out of unconscious identity with the mass? It is . . . called . . . vocation, [which] acts like a law of God. . . . Anyone with a vocation hears the voice of the inner man: he is called."

—*Carl Jung*

Today we look around us and see that the world as we've known it is rapidly shifting. Much dogma that had stuck to us like glue—beliefs we'd never questioned—is peeling off our frozen minds and crumbling around us, along with many of our taken-for-granted institutions, idols, and ideals. And our identities are smashing against walls we can't push through as our old fragmented selves. A "Call to Awaken" to a greater identity is therefore sounding forth, heard by many a restless seeker from inside our own minds and hearts. This Call is coming from the one Soul of Humanity.

Many are beginning to answer this Call, resonating to some faint recollection of a bigger life we've always known deep in our hearts. We're being asked now to take our stand as those who "go first" into the uncarved pathways of our awaiting future. The veil of illusion that's been holding us away from our greater identities and larger lives is being lifted, and we are being asked to pass on through. For perhaps only now are we becoming mature enough to accept the mantle of our rightful heritage as grown-up sons and daughters of God, our Creator, or Cosmic Force.

There are always those who sustain the world by a hidden membership in the true mystical bloodline of brother/sister souls—all here to share in this great awakening. Messengers and fellow travelers already representing a new consciousness are carriers of vision and hope for the ones just coming along. The "Post-Capitalistic Age" is upon us, and we are its harbingers. A new transitional kind of self is about to walk this earth. And we are it!

Even more thrilling still: We are all interrelated with powers greater than we've known before. Divine intelligences and cosmic consciousness enter us through our subjective lives, standing ready—each according to its own quality—to receive power from the order of beings above, while passing it to the order below. And we too, in our small but significant way, are part of this Great Chain of Being.

Beyond Darwin's "survival of the fittest" concept, life seems to grow from within itself. On all levels of nature, we see a continual and purposeful process of evolution from the lesser to the greater. And so, we must each learn to honor this sacred process within ourselves, as active, *wide awake* participants. As we move forward toward something more fulfilling and complete, we outgrow our limitations. Life continually unfolds, it appears, yet the forms or bodies seem to die off only to be reborn or reshaped, forever made new with fresh designs. Although nature is truly wondrous, it has not yet fashioned an eternal form in which we can rest.

All physical bodies dissolve over time. Yet something of value remains, even from the smallest life.

So it is that we are all being called to some kind of awesome "abnormal living," and to the shouldering of a definite responsibility. But don't let this arouse a fear of being pushed into something, for spiritual forces must always await humanity's free will. Never would any higher order infringe upon the divine right of anyone to make his or her own decisions, to exert our individual rights to freedom from any authority not of our own choosing.

True freedom can be practiced only by an enlightened, empowered people—those who would never tolerate authoritarianism in any religion or government. People who are self-realized tell the truth, freely making their own evaluations and decisions. Those who rise to the Call in any generation are this type—ones who are individuating, stepping out of "mass consciousness," eager to think for themselves and to risk new, uncharted ways.

If this message is tugging at your heartstrings, you may be among those who are already programmed to wake up now, and hear the Call of your soul, willing to undergo whatever you must to prepare for the life of spirit to manifest right here on earth.

The coming of the new millennium coincides with the Mayan calendar and a number of other great cycles, together signifying a truly momentous time in history. As English playwright Christopher Fry tells us in *The Sleep of Prisoners*, our affairs are now "soul-sized."

This is the time of accelerated awakening. But we're right where we're supposed to be. Having traveled a long stream of evolutionary change, we've come, one more time, to the start of a new cycle. A New Age—in its legitimate scientific sense—is upon us. And a new kind of life is beginning.

At this great turning of the cosmic wheel, healing ourselves and helping others are two aspects of the same process, and can no longer be separated. It is only by our own willingness to heal and "do the new" that we become it. Only then can we offer to others the courage and conviction gained from our own "personal research," grounded in the actual experience of direct knowing. For we can never guide others into places we've not traveled ourselves.

To make this journey we're called toward, we must have a *living* faith with a *burning* zeal that pierces through the darkness to the center where there is light. Nothing ever really moves without great intensity and intent behind it. Faith is not a concept; it is a *power!* As we are reminded in scripture:

> "Faith is the *substance* of things hoped for,
> the *evidence* of things not seen."
> —*Hebrews XI:1*

Whenever a great human cycle ends, humanity is required to "cap it off" with a balanced heart and clear understanding of what the cycle represented. Then, with lessons learned and psyches healed, we clean the slate for a fresh entry into the coming era, eager to begin anew on a higher rung of evolution's ladder.

Choosing to rise to the Call of the Soul is a privilege that only the brave-hearted in any age would ever attempt, however. Many today have settled for less than who they are—and they are used to this state, content to remain there. But not you, if you are feeling the "divine unrest" to move on! Many *are* intimately aware of Spirit's urgent tug, and are already resonating to the encouraging themes of the times just ahead. And if you've read this far, you are probably one of these eager ones.

So welcome aboard! May the messages in this book help to make your time of awakening safer and more understandable. May you hear them not only for yourselves, but for all those you will serve by your example on the next leg of the long journey Home.

Part 1

As Humanity Evolves . . . .

Just as plants reach toward the sun, we humans
are forever striving for "the light"—the fullness
that is our destiny. At some point we each enter
our true life's path into a wholesome *mature*
place of service in the world, a place where we
can love ourselves and others alike.

Here our Soul shines through us, illuminating
the myriad actions, feelings, and thoughts
of everyday life. We find ourselves among
others who are also traveling a spiritual Path of
Unfolding—expanding beyond the old ways
we've experienced humanity in the past.
And we willingly accept the "growing pains"
that naturally go along with the process of
birthing a new consciousness. We are radiating
Spirit, and this makes our souls light-hearted.

These evolutionary times call for our letting go
of stereotypical ideas and images—so we can
advance toward our spiritual fulfillment with
more integrity and joy. Designing new prototypes,
we are stepping beyond our pasts and moving on.

The Human Condition Is Much Too Conditioned!

How It Got This Way

The "human condition" begins before birth. Every human embryo that takes form within another human's body comes to know difficulties and pain during life's earliest prenatal journey.

Researchers have discovered that while still unborn and pre-verbal, the information-gathering mechanism of the fetus is not the intellect, but the whole being. Physical sensations, feelings, and intuitive perceptions become our teachers as we tiny creatures learn through *experiential* data.*

So babies arrive in the world partially programmed by DNA coding, and conditioned from life in the womb. We're already "imprinted" with our family patterns, both strengths and weaknesses. Yet at this early stage, we are still completely innocent and vulnerable to this life we're seeing for the very first time.

Seeking the nurturing love that is both a birthright and a critical part of survival is our earliest natural preoccupation. We depend on adults—parents and others in authority

---

*For more information, refer to writings about perinatal psychology, such as *The Secret Life of the Unborn Child*, by Thomas Verny, M.D., or the works of Stanislav Grof, M.D., concerning the birth process.

—for the most basic physical and emotional needs. These adults also provide our next layer of conditioning, often by unthinkingly doing what seems right to them, when in truth it may not be right at all.

No matter how well-intentioned, those around us make mistakes that can deeply wound a young psyche. In childhood, and on up through the stages of development, young people learn to adapt to the expectations of others. In the process, they continually deny parts of themselves, becoming less and less aligned with their true selves, their souls.

In Western cultures, where spirituality takes a back seat to an action-oriented society, money and power are more highly valued than compassion or self-awareness. Celebrating ego gratification, society supports an outer-directed focus, the ignorance and greed that are destroying our planet.

Because extended family members often are not geographically near enough to "be there" for each other, children do without the guidance of loving elders and other relatives; they are largely brought up by day-care centers and television. And this scenario is mild compared to seriously dysfunctional homes that produce clinically troubled adults.

It isn't just the Western hemisphere that's suffering, of course. Most modern cultures have their own versions of harmful societal values. Whether they believe "children are to be seen and not heard," "men never cry," or other ideas that undervalue feelings, this type of belief system can be very harmful. It ignores crucial portions of our nature and stifles the probability of the well-adjusted development that leads to creative and fulfilled living.

What is a child to do with its natural childlike spontaneity and joy, or its hurt feelings? These quite human emotions are repressed, to later emerge in some unhealthy kind of denial, whether as a pleasure-seeking self, one hooked on pornography or rebelliousness, or one who is so frightened of feelings that all emotions go dead. And the unexamined but generally accepted false beliefs that can do so much harm are unconsciously passed on from generation to generation. And so, like an epidemic, the denial spreads.

All of this has resulted in the ongoing perpetuation of floundering individuals who have lost their sense of security, well-being, and wholeness (holiness). As isolated separatists, many now have little sense of connection with the earth that feeds them or the force that created them. The focus is much more outside themselves, on competitively "doing," than on the inner worlds of creatively "becoming." It is only when we are cut off from our feelings that we can harm ourselves, another, or our Mother Earth.

The current world situation has deteriorated to such a disastrous state that civilization is being forced to wake up. People around the world are coming to understand their interconnectedness with all other beings, as well as with the land masses and diminishing supplies of air and water. And so, the planet is no longer being taken for granted as a life-sustaining certainty. Many of us are beginning to realize that a monumental "healing" on all levels must take place, and that everyone individually is responsible for making it happen.

In these uncertain times, our extensive negative conditioning is a fact of modern life. It must be recognized and taken seriously before healing can occur. One of the greatest fallacies is the cliche that matter-of-factly states, "Time heals all wounds.'' Looking the other way in neutrality or faking cheerfulness instead of dealing with the problems can only make them worse.

Exercise: Your Personal Human Condition

To make humanity's current plight more personal and real for you, why not stop reading for a few minutes now, and take some time to reflect. You might want to play some soft music, and do this exercise as a meditation.

When you're ready, take a few gentle breaths, and think about the conditions surrounding your birth and the family you were born into. Remember as much detail as possible—how your mother was feeling, how various members of the family prepared for and reacted to your birth, and anything else about the situation. Think about the issues that come from this DNA of yours, both physical and emotional.

After this time of self-reflection, you can expand on the experience by jotting down both the strengths and weaknesses your personal conditioning has given you. Then do an inventory regarding these characteristics you came in with and the conditions you entered. Note how they are affecting your current personal life and your vocation.

For instance: What kinds of models did your family provide (positive or negative) that added to your knowledge of personality development? How have these models helped you build strengths you've needed? Did you have to learn certain skills as a defense against any specific adult? How have these skills helped in your personal growth or your work? What family role did you play growing up that now has new meaning for you as an adult; perhaps a hero, peacemaker, or the ''clown''?

This exercise is good for pointing out a strong and exact connection between your own personal issues and where you can be most effective in helping Humanity heal.

Healing Is *in the Works*

In spite of all the conditioning we humans undergo, our world is not without hope. The inborn urge toward wholeness drives us into "journeys of awakening" and leads to the discovery of our spiritual selves. In the process, connections are re-established with nature, the ways of indigenous peoples, and the mystery of the cosmos. As we awaken, we're acquiring skills and the wisdom to use them for healing the Earth's ills. It helps to always remember that the *Soul is already illumined*; we need only to learn to welcome it, to remove the blocks within us so it can shine through.

Fortunately, we are seeing this revival of the human spirit now everywhere we go, even as so many of our older institutions are collapsing around us. A shift *is* taking place, as past views are finally being challenged. Signs are emerging to indicate that a reversal is currently underway, a shift that has begun to correct the devastating effects of so much conditioning.

For quite some time now, the general public has been rejecting widespread misrepresentations of truth, such as politically filtered news stories. And while this type of broadcast is being spurned, an increasing number of other shows address issues such as: improved communications for developing healthy interpersonal relationships; environmental awareness for restoring and protecting the planet;

the humane works of teachers like the Dalai Lama and Mother Teresa; and powerful self-healing techniques for physical ailments of all kinds.

These changes of emphasis are partly due to the fast-paced Western civilization's increased respect for the ancient spiritual traditions. For example, Chinese acupuncture and various energy models of healing are slowly penetrating our health care systems in the West. Herbal medicine and vitamin/mineral supplements are now widely used in addition to prescription drug therapies. And meditation is being appreciated for its ability to bring us back to our true selves. Transcending cultural and religious barriers, meditation has the exact opposite effect of a life filled with aggressive competition, which is intent on achievement and amassing possessions. Meditation and inner reflection teach how insignificant all our grasping really is.

Myths offer another example of a renewed interest in pre-modern ways. People everywhere are now rediscovering the oldest stories on record, and learning about the symbolism in the myths' time-honored themes. From them we can learn much about ourselves, and find hope by dressing these timeless heroic tales in modern clothes, as we apply their universal truths to make our everyday lives more meaningful. These old stories are our true heritage, reminding us that we are mythic beings ourselves.

Meditation, myths, and processes such as guided imagery deal with the inner life, where we can access the wisdom of our hearts. From within, rather than focusing on other people's opinions and material ''outer'' things, we learn to listen for messages from our souls, messages about our bigger stories. Trusting our deepest feelings and intuition (working with subjective images, flashes of inspiration, and dreams, for example) gradually provides this access to inner wisdom, and leads to the consciousness raising that is so badly needed in these times.

Exercise: **Your Own Mythical Character**

[AUTHOR ANECDOTE FROM JACQUELYN] *To give you an idea about relating to the myths, here's an example: At one juncture in my life, I found myself in love with two men at once—a fatherly Arthurian type and a romantic Lancelot. And I realized that I was playing out a "Guinevere" story line. This awareness brought me much insight, and also a badly needed warning.*

Stop for a while now and reflect on a mythical character you feel attracted to, or who reminds you of yourself. This may be easier if you first select a current pattern in your life, then think about any myths that parallel it. Draw on whatever legends you're familiar with—from literature, religious tradition, childhood fairy tales, the classical mythology of Greece, Egypt, etc.

Once you've decided on a myth that fits, focus on the details of the story—specific characters, their actions and attitudes, and the conditions or challenges present. See how your own situation simulates the ancient tale.

This self-reflection should provide some clarity about how you've been playing out your role. You may see how this mythical aspect is enhancing your life, or recognizing it may help prevent an outcome you'd regret.

The evolutionary cycle we're moving into is considered by many to be an "Age of Synthesis." This means that healing the human condition will require a spirituality that recognizes all living things as unique parts of a greater whole.

"Unity in diversity" is our keynote for the coming times. This kind of spirituality encompasses a return to the ancient wisdom of natural laws, compassion for fellow beings in all their differences and conditions, and respect for the inner truth that humanity instinctively knows at its core. The great psychologist Carl Jung talked about a paradox, which goes like this: Though we are each unique, we can never separate from our universal roots without risking a grave neurosis. We are connected to these larger patterns in the psyche as strongly as the organs are connected to our physical bodies!

To effect a global healing at this critical time in history, we would do well to learn a lesson from Buddhism. According to its teachings, enlightenment is achieved through *the unconditioned*, that which flows freely. To move forward now, we must align with our own truths, great and small, rather than being dulled by all the pre-conditioned "unreality" that has created this current human robotic predicament.

Becoming Soul-Centered

Welcoming the Divine Mediator

Your soul is peeking out through your eyes, wondering if it is safe here to come through. Humanity's Soul is that one in whom we live and move and have our Being. Your SOUL is the sensual/sensory, conscious apparatus of Spirit entering through your five physical senses, your mind, and your heart, to experience life here on this earth consciously. When not embodied through people like us, the one Soul lives in its own dimension, a place so beyond time and space that we can hardly imagine it while here in human form. Yet we can each recognize and experience our individual souls as we learn to embody them. For, as unity in diversity, we each have an individual soul.

The Soul is a mediator between spirit and matter, a divine Child of Father/Mother God. Your soul is who perceives your reality with spirit. It is the *quality* of everything in life, the *essence* of every experience. And as such, it affects all three realms of earthly existence: the mental, emotional and physical life.

Mentally your soul is what gives the situations in your life their sense of meaning and sacred purpose. It is your consciousness. At those precious times when you are living out some ordinary event and suddenly become aware of its greater significance, your soul is dominating your mind, bringing you clarity.

Emotionally your soul is your heart's bliss—a mixture of love, compassion, intense yearnings, awe-struckness, jubilance, tender-heartedness, gratitude, wonder, and woes. It feels deeply, appreciating greatly anything to do with relatedness, sacred purpose and life. Your soul may have you reaching out to another in compassion and a heartfelt desire to connect, to *really* connect.

Physically your soul lights up your eyes and puts a lilt in your voice, as it whisks you into moments of intense delight. It urges you into playful activity and expressions of joyful inspiration and childlike curiosity. Your soul is what adds intensity to any of your physical senses.

The highest, most fulfilling way we can live in this world is with our souls totally involved on all three levels—mental, emotional, and physical. The individual soul's outward expression happens through our egos, as these two elements in us maintain an ongoing, uniquely important relationship to each other.*

We all together make up one collective soul of Humanity. Because of this, no matter how much we suffer, we individually are *never* our conditions! By its very nature, the Soul of Humanity is here to constantly remind us of what is essential and real.

Your **PSYCHE** is your individual soul's mirrored reflection. And Humanity's Psyche is the Collective Unconscious Mind, which mirrors our species' universal Soul. Reflecting your soul, your psyche is a mediator between Spirit and

---

*Ego is fully discussed in Part 2, under *Our Many Selves*, beginning on page 64.

Matter, your own personal way of knowing anything at all. Without our psyches, we could not *conceive* of anything, not even God. Nor could we *perceive* anything from our physical senses, or truly feel it either.

Our psyches register the essence or quality of everything created and not created. Without them, we would all be indiscriminate cosmic "blobs," experiencing everything at once, and therefore nothing at all.

SPIRIT is abstract, formless, undifferentiated energy, which *inspires* us. When we let it in, Spirit becomes a force that turns us on, and moves us toward the realization of our inner Ideal, that which we hope to become at least a facsimile of. As spiritual beings in human form, this is always our deepest yearning.

Psyche, your soul's mirror, is your consciousness-maker. What we can make conscious gives us power over our lives. But what is left unconscious has power over us—and will "come upon us like Fate" until we recognize and take responsibility for what is living inside us, motivating our thoughts, feelings, and actions.

As we shift from ego-driven separatist consciousness to becoming soul-centered personalities, we must get to know our psyches well—making conscious the images we carry around in our minds, and how we think and feel. For without good psychological health, we create a bogus spirituality that can only masquerade as "high" or "whole." As we go through the processes that awaken the psyche, we feel aligned with Spirit once more; we feel we've come Home. This is certainly a "project" worth pursuing. Wouldn't you agree?

Seeking True Community—
the Communion of Souls

Many people today are yearning to feel "at Home" once more. This does not necessarily mean they are looking for a fixed community that maintains a particular identity or demands a certain loyalty; rather, they seek others who see a similar vision and hold a common intention—one of aligning their personal lives with their soul's purpose for having been born. A strong instantaneous rapport with all who come together in such gatherings creates a cohesive sense of community no matter where these groups are formed, and regardless of how much or little time they spend together.

As we all commit to this process of awakening to higher levels of human functioning, our past becomes integrated, and our future stands revealed; we live in the moment, in what we discover to be the ultimate Now. This happens more easily in the loving company of others. As we mature, we cast away our old habits that no longer serve us, while retaining the goodness of our earlier expressions—with a sense of ease and a resilience gained from the wisdom of our experiences. Sharing in this process is the true "communion of souls."

Perhaps you have the ability to draw together such gatherings, large or small, to give some souls a place to "commune." If so, following up on it would be a worthy venture.

As the old drops away and the new begins to take shape through each of us, we will recognize that we are indeed living within our greater family of Humanity as one soul, and that we need each other. For healing ourselves, advancing forward, and helping to guide others to do so as well are all the same process. Being a guide cannot be separated from being a seeker.

A path of Self-knowledge and Self-mastery cannot be learned from outer experts; the Soul, our greater Self, is the only Teacher, and the Self resides within us all. So whether we are the ones wanting help or the ones who are helping, we must all enter "the path" that leads us inward toward the depths of the human psyche. Upon this subjective inner terrain we meet the Soul.

This inner journey is not always smooth or effortless, however; to expect it to be so is an illusion. It's quite easy to "pull out of true," either falling backwards into a state of inertia and old habits, or moving too rapidly into an ungrounded speculation.

A widespread frustration and sense of futility can strongly permeate our consciousness as we begin moving away from the old and on into the emerging new creation. The Hand of God will sometimes even bring a disaster that functions like a giant broom, sweeping away all distractions and obstructions in the path of our greatest good.

Finding the tension between all the opposing extremes we encounter, and learning to abide there in the tension as we move through these accelerated times is the new way of being—at least for now. So guides and fellow seekers are needed and sought. Otherwise the journey is too difficult, and many lose their way. Since it is our nature to be forever on the move—inwardly, if not outwardly—there is no place to rest for a species such as ours: This journey itself is our Home!

As guides on the journey, our spiritual quest requires a balance between speaking our truths and knowing when not to. Discretion is important, to spare ourselves energy spent with those who are likely to ridicule. Still, when we remain silent, we may miss the opportunity to discover how ready many others are to discuss such matters. There *is* a Power greater than ourselves and a Plan greater than our daily appointment books can hold! And we are being asked to rise to this Call, to demonstrate this spiritual activity we were born to express. Our time to come on out and be ourselves has arrived. We must refuse to hide any longer.

As spiritual beings inhabiting human bodies, we are entering a time of fulfillment, a blossoming for many of our kind. This is an evolutionary fact—and no small feat! It means we will know and experience ourselves in a whole new way, anchored as a new type of consciousness "upon a new floor of our mansion." We will experience a *felt* awareness and stabilization as being our fully realized selves. Isn't this what you've always wanted—to just be your Self—with no more pretense, no more trying to be someone you're not, no more feeling lost in space without purpose or dream?

Birthing a New Consciousness

Invisible Influences

When we begin an ascension in consciousness, we start awakening to our larger patterns; we merge with the "archetypal" reality. The Greek word "archos" means *first* or *root*. An **ARCHETYPE** is a model for all things of the same kind or "type," the perfect example of it, a pattern or blueprint for anything we can imagine. An archetype then is the image and "psychic feeling" we have about the whole nature of something. Everything in manifestation has its archetype.

Universal archetypes portray the many "character" possibilities available to us from the vast collective unconscious mind of Humanity, by providing holistic patterns of all the Ideals for any new form of life as it evolves. An illustration is the way in which many today are learning from the archetypes of King/Queen, Warrior, Magician, and Lover, based on the work of Jungian psychoanalyst Robert Moore. Other common "person" archetypes are Mother, Father, Child, Partner or Mate, Leader, Tyrant, Savior, Perpetrator, Victim, Lost Soul, Wise Old Man or Woman, God, Goddess, etc.

Besides these personages, archetypes can also be universal processes, such as Matrimony, Transformation, Birth, Death, and Individuation, or pure qualities—like Wisdom, Love, Generosity, and Dedication. The list is virtually endless. (Notice that names of archetypes are capitalized.)

When something moves toward the pure expression of itself, it is said to be "archetypal." The archetype of whatever it is influences us, often without our conscious awareness, and can help us to evolve toward wholeness by impacting us with a big "dose" of its pure characteristics. We begin to envision or long for the Ideal of something. We focus on it with full intention. And eventually, it takes shape, or is "realized" through us as its representatives here in physical form. Thus, the unconscious mind becomes conscious when we are open to receiving the gifts of the archetypes, as they are our blueprints for being fully human.

The Divine Feminine

One archetype that is especially prominent at this current evolutionary time is the Divine Feminine, which is receptive, intuitive, and inclusive. The past millennium became so imbalanced with its "hardened masculine," patriarchal, and aggressive ways that the Divine Feminine is being called in to help restore balance.

This is evidenced as people report apparitions of the Virgin Mary, or feelings of connection to Sophia, the pre-Christian lost Goddess of Wisdom, the original Bride of God. Others are hearing Gaia, the living and sacred Earth, as she cries out to them. And "Goddess energy" appears as a theme on many greeting cards and workshop brochures.

The archetypal process of Birth is trying to rectify itself too, with collective issues such as abortion and adoption becoming commonplace on the evening news. These are some of the feminine themes that are strongly influencing the shape of the new consciousness. As this feminine energy begins to circulate once more, we regain our respect for Mother Earth and our purposeful human process.

A note about the use of "feminine": It's important not to confuse Maculine and Feminine *Principles* with the subject of gender. This is not a sexist issue. We all have within us both assertive drives (Masculine) and receptive drives (Feminine). Equally important, one expresses itself by moving outward, the other by drawing inward.

So the Masculine and Feminine Principles have nothing to do with sexual preferences or in-the-flesh romantic relationships. When these contra-sexual Principles merge, a marriage of mind and heart results, all within one person. And as we move into the Age of Synthesis, we'll drop our "gender issues," recognizing both Principles within each of us.

EXERCISE: **Your Current Archetypal Theme**

As we travel along our own evolutionary paths, we can help our clients and friends get in touch with the archetypes that are impacting them. Viewing our lives and personal development through a lens of archetypal themes brings understanding and a sense of wholeness to the multiple and seemingly unconnected strings of events in our lives. Here's a guided imagery to serve this aim:

Settle into a comfortable position where you won't be disturbed, and relax as much as you can. Close your eyes and take a few gentle breaths. Feel yourself moving into a non-time space, as you gradually let go of this earthly reality for a while.

Now, in your mind's eye, allow yourself to see an image of the overriding Theme or archetypal Person controlling your current state of being. Let this image appear spontaneously.

When the Image comes, notice how it wants to relate to you. Be open to its appearance and motions, noticing if it gives you a message, a symbol, or some other sign. Just allow the inner Image to unfold. . . . Take some time to appreciate the Image who appeared, thank it, and create an ending for this inner scene that is satisfying to you.

Now gradually come back into this reality, and reflect on what just happened inside your own mind. You may want to write or draw something to capture the experience, or simply reflect in silence for a while.

The Challenge Ahead

As planetary citizens inhabiting our precarious Earth, we are charged now with the awesome responsibility to begin seeing it all—ourselves included—quite differently than we did before. The new concepts involved here come from both psychology and physics, and are borne out by the teachings of most spiritual paths. For the major transformation of birthing a new consciousness, two evolutionary shifts are required of us.

1) To resolve our difficulties with the concept of **DUAL-ISM**: We must make the shift from a limiting "either/or" way of thinking to a "both/and" acceptance of all life has to offer, both the pleasant and the painful; we need to accept all parts of ourselves rather than hating one part while loving another.

   Since "oppositeness" is our very nature, we

must learn to work with this inherent dynamic of dualism, appreciating all the pairs of opposites within us as *complementary* rather than contradictory. For it takes two of anything to create a "fire by friction" that makes something "third" and higher.

The Law of Complementarity in physics validates this view by stating that an atom behaves as both particle and wave, which demonstrates their opposite functions; yet the *whole* atom contains both. This is duality within unity.*

2) To release creative expression: We must make the shift from a disease-based psychology to a spiritual psychology; that is, instead of symptoms being viewed as shameful dysfunctions and pathological, they are seen as factors required for birthing a new life.

This approach releases us from low self-esteem, while putting us back in touch with our creative soul powers and spiritual purpose.

In a nutshell, to be contemporary thinkers, we have to focus on dissolving all splits by seeing the value in either side, and let go of our judgment—to stop judging *ourselves* as well as others. Then we must have the courage to come on out from behind our walls of fear, mistrust, and low self-esteem, and express our unique creativity, however that seems the most natural—to just relax and practice being ourselves. Then one day we'll look around and see that we've indeed stepped into our real Self.

---

*Dualism is discussed further in Part 2, under *The Heart Is the Bridge*, page 56.

Working with an Unacceptable Part of Yourself

Take some time now to stop and reflect on a part of yourself you cannot stand! Bring it up into your conscious awareness and name it. . . . Now let it show you its gift, its positive or helpful attribute.

Spend a little time being with this aspect of yourself. And if you can, give it some love or appreciation, and stay with that for a while. Let yourself really feel a new acceptance happening in your body.

As Physics Sees It

The main difference between the dying and emerging world views is this: In the old way, we thought we were standing apart from the evolutionary process, irrelevant objects in space being acted upon by a greater force. When out of sorts, we thought we could go to experts, give them our allegiance, and be "repaired" like mechanical clocks.

Today, however, subatomic physics takes a different view, which aids us in building a more accurate psychology. From studying the very basis of ourselves, we're finding that we are a part of the evolutionary process, not separate from it; and we are influencing our own creation. This exacting science of subatomic realities has determined that in observing a piece of data, *our very act of observation itself changes the data.*

In other words, an atom occupies an infinite number of positions simultaneously, *until an observer sees the atom.* This tells us that *how* we observe creates the reality we perceive, and that the mind of the observer is more significant than the object observed!

The implications of this finding are profound concerning the nature of reality, and the nature of human beings. It seems that we have a powerful **CO-CREATING** role in our own evolution, which depends on what we choose to focus on, to recognize, or to call "real." We've been living in the middle of our own picture unaware of the part we play in creating what we think of as "reality."

To reiterate: From the scientific perspective of physics, we consider "real" and believe in only those things we select from the pool of all possibilities and put our emotional energy behind. Since our *observation* is what co-creates our personal reality at every moment, individual consciousness itself is creative, and we are the reality-makers; only *we* attribute meaning to our experiences.*

Further, a number of minds thinking alike can change our common (consensual) reality. Just as disagreeing minds split up the world, minds that agree with each other unite it. Therefore, when a group of people together all believe in a similar world view, a consensual realitiy manifests, and they label it "the way of life."

You might want to stop for a minute and reflect on your current life situation, and discover what you have been calling "real." This makes for a great self-awareness exercise.

*Our role of co-creation is discussed further, as it relates to *Invocation*, on page 108.

Recognizing "Re-cognition"

Besides establishing that *what we recognize* as a real possibility *creates our reality*, the new physics says that "parallel universes" exist (or parallel realities)—where time loses its meaning—and that the mental process necessary for merging these parallel universes is *recognition*.

To *recognize* is to "re-cognize"—which connotes a remembrance of something we already know at the soul level. It is our soul's way of cognizing. *Recognition* always brings us an "Aha!"—the sense of a bigger meaning that carries purpose.

To effect the recognition or "seeing things differently," which is necessary for birthing a new consciousness, we must create special environments for Spirit to come through, for it is our guiding force. Remember, Spirit moves us toward the realization of our Ideal.

The required **SACRED SPACE** is a loving atmosphere (usually in a group) where people feel nurtured and totally safe to be themselves, and to work on their inner healing processes. The space is clean, everything in it is purposeful, and reminders of our spiritual nature are evidenced by artwork, symbols, amulets, and overall simplicity.*

In sacred space, held steady by a soul-centered guide and a focused spiritual intent, Spirit enters; all judgment and either/or fixations are dropped and the bigger picture (or meaning) is seen. And research has shown that when judgment is absent, creativity flourishes.

*Guidelines on how to create sacred space are given in Appendix 1, page 211.

Those doing transformational inner work are reminded that they are here on earth to take on the human condition as part of their souls' intentions for incarnation. They come together in sacred space to look inward for answers to their deepest questions, and relax into whatever emotions come up for them. Here, with no fear of criticism, they experience the "let-gos" of all the excess baggage they've collected along life's way.

We all need to grieve our losses, own our wounds and consequential imbalances, and forgive them. In the safety of loving groupwork, we can together learn to heal. Further, we can nurture our subjective dreams and all the visions of the future that are making our hearts truly sing. This is where Spirit brings us the transformational tasks of purification, integration, and envisioning, whenever we complete a human cycle in the Great Chain of Being.

When committed to our own healing, we are all planetary workers. Taking on our individual issues and making them conscious is how we heal them—not only for ourselves, but for all of Humanity as one soul. For everything we do in life is more than just personal; *never forget this!* All events have their archetypal roots tying them to the collective. When any one of us becomes a little lighter, we've helped lighten Humanity's one body.

Therefore, any troublesome issue we can access personally, and feel through and release, helps not only us but all others who have had this same problem in living; we are "doing our part" to help clear the entire energy field of this disturbance. The context surrounding our troubles and pain is thereby broadened and given a larger sacred purpose as well as its personal meaning.

Our spiritual nature is a psychological fact! Roberto Assagioli, M.D., who developed the psychology known as Psychosynthesis, wrote ''. . . in so far as these phenomena—whether termed spiritual, mystical, or parapsychological—change the inner reality and the outer behavior of an individual, they are real . . .'' Dr. Assagioli goes on to say, ''. . . the spiritual Self is the greatest reality, the real essence of our being.'' So, you see, our spirituality *is* the real and transformative force that empowers our lives. To deny this core nature of ours is to deny our very selves.

Part 2

The Quickening Process
• Our Work of Transformation •

Everyone is evolving. For growth toward
maturity is the nature of life itself. As we rise
to the Soul's Call to awaken, however, we enter
onto an *accelerated* path of spiritual evolution.
So, for some of us, inner processes activate,
spinning us through experiences so rapidly that
our whole identity shifts. This process has been
known by mystics of all Ages as "the quickening."

This is our sacred work of transformation,
which redefines how we look at the concept
of "work." Rather than drudgery, work is now
the *inner* work we do on ourselves—the *real*
work of life, our Self-creation. It overflows into
serving the common good, and its automatic
offshoot is the thrill of knowing we're moving
forward toward wholeness.

This process requires deep reflection and
observation, often by-passing or expanding
beyond the intellect. We learn "the Work" by
steadily gaining a sense of what is really true
for us behind "the world of appearances" and
all the limitations of our ordinary lives. Then
we develop the courage to live as these qualities
of truth, and model this authenticity for others.
Becoming authentic is the key, and our only goal.

Opening to the Mystery— Redefining the Work

Evolving toward our human potential doesn't mean struggling to learn massive amounts of new information. It means developing a different sense of the world and its people, one that's more accepting, or *less* defined. And this means honoring the wisdom already within us, our authenticity.

At this stage of humanity's unfolding, our symptoms are no longer considered disease, dysfunction, bad, or wrong. Instead, they are seen as signs of these evolutionary times, the "growing pains" necessary for the process of birthing a new consciousness.

This is about trusting ourselves and opening to mystery, rather than closely following formulas, trying to remember what rule or category applies to everything around us. In a very real sense, striving for our own wholeness—and helping others to reach theirs—often requires a lot of forgetting!

And so the new-consciousness shift in thinking challenges a number of concepts previously considered basic to healing and helping others.

This chapter explains the more open and receptive approach now emerging that will serve people in the healing professions. And remember, these concepts apply not only to therapists but to *all* others who are striving toward wholeness as well.

• • •

In the context of this book, **NEW WORLD VIEW** refers to the evolutionary ways of thinking pertinent to our times. In relation to the health professions, it means an emerging style of counseling that honors the wisdom within clients, rather than believing the therapist is "the expert" on another. The new world view shifts our focus inwardly, and leads to self-awareness, self-responsibility, and self-empowerment.* The new therapies offer guidance and support for following an inner path of direct experience, which leads to direct knowledge. On a path of direct knowledge, the Self is our only guide and can be accessed only from within.

• • •

Modern psychology talks a lot about **ADDICTION**, but it too is taking on an expanded meaning. In the new world view, the expression "addictive living" encompasses all types of human imbalances—our various addictions and attachments to the many aspects of the entire human condition.

Every one of us is viewed as having some form of compulsivity—obsessions, biases, or attachments that cause us to become lopsided or "out of sync" with others or even with varying aspects of ourselves. In fact, in our "humanness," many of us have become addicted to suffering or to negativity itself! **ADDICTION** then is the person's out-of-bal-

---

*This concept is discussed further in the next chapter, titled *A Closer Look at the New World View*.

ance condition, whatever form it takes. Whenever we become lopsided, fanatical, or extremist in any manner whatsoever, this is a clear sign that we are moving "off the mark." And all of us must discover and own these imbalances in ourselves; our spiritual growth cannot come from "labels" laid on us by "experts," as was so often the case in this current closing cycle.

• • •

Similarly, **RECOVERY** is no longer a term limited to people living in sobriety or abstinence from a specifically defined addiction. The term has been broadened to mean *recovery from an imbalanced human condition*. Without the imbalance, we can live from our "center."* And, as we heal, the idea of *recovery* gradually shifts to *discovery* of the true Self. This represents a turn away from focusing on the past, toward a focus on an emerging future and greater life.

Our recovery (toward balance) is a retrieval of the parts of ourselves that have gotten lost in the debilitating circumstances of living. We recognize that suffering, stress, conflicts, ignorance, and pain are integral parts of being human, obstacles each of us must endure, which often lead to problems of imbalance. And our past must be dealt with and healed before we can move on.

• • •

*The concept of "center" is discussed further under *Living from Center*, page 103.

So who are the new **HEALERS**? The therapist of the future realizes that we're all in need of healing, not from just one or two uncomplicated symptoms, but from having gotten caught up in the throes of the multi-faceted, paradoxical, and alluring human condition! Because of this, a healer is no longer thought of as an "outside expert," one who has all the answers for a client. Rather, therapists know they too are journeying toward wholeness, and that they can often guide others while learning from their clients as well. *Outer experts have no place on a path of direct knowledge!* So all must be the kind of guides who lead people back to their own inner wisdom. We must develop qualities and skills that settle down our egos and teach us to be empowering of others. All goals in therapy should support this aim, rather than trying to solve the clients' problems. And any kind of "treatment plan" must remain dynamic and open-ended, never static.

In a sense, the new healers are resonators, who compassionately listen and reflect back what they've heard, then model their faith in the process of transformation. This inspires clients to believe in their own possibilities and to take action for achieving them.

When the deepest healing happens for either client or therapist, it comes from *direct experience in the present moment*, not from analyzing or *talking about* our issues. A detectable energy exchange takes place, a *felt* shift.*

●　●　●

*Healers are discussed further in Part 3, under *People-Helpers*, page 167.

The **THERAPEUTIC STYLE** of individual counseling is giving way toward *connectedness*. One-on-one talk therapy is being replaced more and more by experiential methodologies, including the community experience of groupwork, which is guided by leaders who honor the group process.

Today's trend in psychotherapy is the integration of mind, body, and emotions, replacing the "compartmentalization" so evident in the medical-model approach. Walls between the helper and those needing help are also becoming more pliable, relaxing rigid role behaviors. Helpers are becoming more open-hearted, less formal, and willing to tell their own stories of healing and transformation. This empowers clients and gives them models who are traveling the journey with them as elder brothers and sisters, who are not pretending to be perfect or think they have "arrived."

Community programs learn to honor each participating member's unique contribution. These are synthesis groups: "Unity in diversity" is a very rich experience, so all religious and/or psychological systems are welcome. Though groups need leaders, leadership isn't a "fixed" position. When the connectedness of all is honored, no one's special strength or talent goes to waste. A dynamic flow exists among the involved individuals, where all can express their own true creativity.

• • •

Each of the previous psychological "schools" (Freudian, then Behavioral, and later Humanistic) began as a reaction to the one before it. Now these three earlier modalities have led up to a fourth, Transpersonal psychology, and the even broader category of "spiritual" psychologies, which take in both the ego and the soul. Since "trans" means both *through* and *beyond*, the word "transpersonal" refers to the personal but also moves beyond it, carrying us into more expanded realms of consciousness, such as the mythical and archetypal.

The process of **PSYCHOSPIRITUAL INTEGRATION** developed at Eupsychia is a form of spiritual psychology. A thorough discussion of this term could fill an entire book by itself. But since it appears in this one, an abbreviated explanation is important here.

Just as physical health is never "enough" unless it's accompanied by a basic sense of contentment (feeling fulfilled), psychological well-being reaches a joyous state of completion only when inner peace goes with it. This inner peace comes from sensing and appreciating that one's life, even its mistakes and wrong turns, has meaning and a sacred purpose.

PSYCHOSPIRITUAL INTEGRATION is the blending of a *psycho*logical well-being and a *spirit*ual essence into one whole individual who can function as an integrated Self. Wholeness occurs when both *psychological* principles (relating to the ego) and *spiritual* principles (soul) come together. Psychospiritual Integration begins to happen naturally when the personality and soul meet, each honoring the other for its natural way of being. And this meeting happens in the heart. Therefore, guides for this type of work must be open-hearted people.

The mental health field has come to recognize the need to integrate our egos, and most spiritual paths believe in ego transcendence. The spiritual psychologies teach us we cannot transcend an ego we've never integrated; that is, we cannot move beyond anything we've not adequately made conscious, developed, and healed. A healthy psyche is just as "spiritual" as the soul, since our psyche is our soul's mirrored reflection. And our spiritual essence is just as much a part of the healing as psychological practices.

The combination of the two allows us to live as our whole (holy) selves—spiritual beings involved in the human condition. Psychospiritual Integration merges the logical scientific findings of modern thinking with ancient wisdom, which emphasizes intuition, dream work, revelations, inspirations, spiritual practices, and other elements of the unconscious mind and inner life.

Psychospiritual Integration deals with the *curative* arts— those processes that activate and involve the whole Self in therapeutic work. Methods such as musical guided imagery, mandala drawing, mask making, working with clay and sand trays, sacred ritual, psychodrama, myth making, movement, breathwork, group chanting, singing, and play are all aspects of the curative arts.

By honoring our innate wholeness, Psychospiritual Integration becomes a "psychology of completion" for ending an old cycle and making fresh beginnings.*

• • •

A fundamental premise of Psychospiritual Integration, that spirit is important *because* we are spiritual beings, leads

---

*Psychospiritual Integration is discussed further in Part 3, under *Schools of Psychology*, page 167.

to another basic concept for the healers of the future: Human beings have an innate urge toward personal growth, to evolve through deeper self-knowledge and to feel that they are valuable elements within the grand scheme of things. We all have a built-in inner drive that moves us toward our full awakening and natural expression.

Just as plants turn toward the sun, we naturally feel compelled to keep moving "toward the light" for our own blossoming as a person, evolving toward our species' fruition. We somehow sense our interconnectedness with the universe and all its creatures. It is perfectly natural for us to want to open up to our divine or higher nature, to transcend mundane life, to *become whole.*

This inborn craving for wholeness relates to holiness, since we are spiritual beings in human form. **CONSCIOUS-NESS** is the relation between an inner psychic (spiritual) content and the ego's intellectual understanding of it. Much is said in this book about expanding our consciousness, awakening to our whole selves, and helping others to do the same. The words "consciousness," "awakening," and "transformation" refer to the ongoing human pursuit toward completion, the ultimate healing, which results in wholeness.

A Closer Look at
the New World View

Though you've already read a definition of **NEW WORLD VIEW**, this chapter goes deeper into its exploration. Since a "world view" underlies everything in life, it becomes the foundation on which we make our assumptions.

When a *new* world view emerges, it adds a whole new level to our understanding of human nature by recognizing the higher, more essential core issues. Developments inherent to the process of evolution bring about dramatic changes in the way we think. For instance, we once believed the world was flat, and we based all our assumptions about reality on this premise. Then we discovered the world to be round. So all our old assumptions required a radical re-examination; some even had to be thrown out.

This is what is occurring today in all fields of human endeavor: a new world view has dawned, an evolutionary potential that says we are more than what we appear to be. As mentioned earlier, we used to think that we were separate from others, like physical objects floating around in space, isolated and alone. This made us competitive, and we learned about ourselves by comparison.

Now, looking through a lens of the expanded view of the Soul, we see that we are all parts of an interconnected whole, and we can no longer pit ourselves against one another, whether as persons or as whole nations. Life, according to the new physics, is relationship, fluctuation, and dynamic flow. And our conscious participation in creation, *including our own*, is the vital key to our well-being as human souls.

We are either consciously or unconsciously affecting our own lives. And because we are intricately connected in the web of all creation, we have within us all the wisdom that has ever been, already encoded in our DNA. The implications of this new way of viewing human nature and our place in the universe are staggering. We're forced to wake up and become responsible for what we think, feel, and set into motion.

Yet today we are mostly still operating through ego-based psychologies that see us as mechanical objects needing to be "fixed." Our programs and policies, even our interactions with each other, still basically reflect the old ways, though they no longer seem to be working; nor do they fulfill us. Our Selfhood is expanding beyond these old forms.

Like fish trying to live in a stagnant pool, we are beginning to starve. And since we are spiritual beings, it's spiritual food that we crave! Gradually, people are stepping out, and beginning to honor their new insights and discoveries concerning human nature—*our* nature and core Self.

Taking It More Personally

This is so significant, it bears reiteration: In the old world view we depended on "specialists" in all areas of our lives to define us, and to tell us how to be. We've sought formulas, doctrines, prescriptions, labels, and advice about how to know ourselves, how to be saved, how to heal, how to find sanity, success, health, and spirituality.

Now we're learning not to look for outside experts. And this is quite a shock! Tentatively, and with some trepidation, we are starting to question things, to turn inward to listen to our own hearts and intuition, to unite with the truth of our own being.

In the old way, we thought we were sick, immature, or neurotic when experiencing symptoms of pain, imbalance, or emotional discomfort. We gave ourselves labels of pathology. Now we realize that our personal issues and painful symptoms are products of life's hard lessons, not pathological at all. They are the natural effects of *birthing a new consciousness*. Who does not realize that birth is painful? It places us right at an intersection between life and death!

As a species transmuting into a whole new way of being, it is gradually dawning on us that we have nothing to feel shame about, no one to blame. We are simply a part of the human condition and a ''bigger story,'' one that has a deep sense of collective meaning and purpose as one Humanity. And since we're a species not yet fully evolved, we're behaving as unfinished humans behave. We've made wrong turns, and grown a little gnarl or two, even sometimes gotten completely off-track—usually while doing the best we can.

Marilyn Ferguson, author of *The Aquarian Conspiracy*, compared this shift in consciousness to the way we were as children when looking at those little books that said ''find the missing picture.'' Remember? You'd stare at a tree branch, then suddenly a face or a pair of scissors would jump out! Before, they were invisible.

Because consciousness shifts happen in the mind, they can be instantaneous. Our minds have, in fact, been preparing for the change while we were going about our ordinary business, looking the other way.

How Healing Happens

Today's Task at the Shifting of an Age

As awakening souls, we realize our true nature is buried underneath old programming and old wounds. So we commit to consistently doing inner work, which clears our psyches of the past, and helps *keep* us clear. This is good preparation for helping others, and moving on into the new era with a clean slate.

Once we are better able to live without distortions from our own past wounds, we are in an excellent position to guide others who need healing and are experiencing the throes of transformation. For how can counselors expect to guide clients through excavations into inner space until they've traveled there themselves?

So the new people-helpers are those who consider themselves wounded healers, who have "walked the walk" and can now "talk the talk." Those who guide others are the ones who have gone first. They are no better, just running ahead of the pack. After testing the waters, they stand holding open a safe and heart-felt space for the others to come on through.

Cleansed of much of their past hurts, these new helpers are open to the process with a deep sense of faith and obvious inspiration. They no longer wear their feelings on their sleeves, and have developed a tough resolve to trust the process no matter how rough the seas of change become. Then, as guides, they are able to maintain an attitude of receptivity, compassion, courage, and hope for those undergoing their own personal transformations.

In order to access both aspects of their nature (ego and soul) so that complete healing can occur, the new breed of people-helpers works with the unconscious as well as the conscious mind. For although healing in the outer, problem-solving arena can come from the more ordinary means of rational thinking and discussion, this isn't enough. Non-ordinary states of consciousness—such as meditation, guided imagery, and breathwork may offer—must also be utilized to access and heal our deeper subjective lives. Both the ego (our outer self) and the soul (inner self) must be involved.

The healing of dysfunctional or unhealthy living happens in two ways, and often simultaneously:

1) We return to the past to reach, understand, and heal our fragmented selves and the wounded emotions that were created by negative family patterns, or any other undigested pieces of our personal past.

   In a therapy session, this might look like a client falling into a regressive state, crying and raging about a childhood pain while simultaneously reliving the abusive situation *as a felt experience*.

And . . .

2) We open to a future, more integrated, and higher identity that is available within our consciousness, one that is connected to the whole. Learning to focus on this higher Self, we discover through practice how

to take in its greater identity as real. We learn to *be* this expanded self.

For example, a woman undergoing a healing might suddenly ''see'' with her inner eye all the mothers in the world who have had similar painful experiences, and feel identified with all these mothers.

Then an image of the Divine Mother (an archetype) may soothe the woman from within, while a deep insight or resolution takes place.

In this manner, our personal and transpersonal lives merge and expand us. This type of experience can happen in a non-ordinary state of consciousness, but rarely (if ever) occurs during ordinary talk therapy. When we can see beyond our personal pain into its archetypal dimension, we are healed; the entire issue has been experienced, felt, understood, and integrated. Now it is completed, no longer a needed lesson.

The task at hand is to honor all aspects of our nature, shadow/light, past/future, ego/soul, personal/transpersonal; and to see that all are sacred and come from the whole.

The Cross as a Symbol

The Cross can be used as a symbol to demonstrate the difference between ordinary and non-ordinary consciousness. The horizontal line or ''arm'' of the Cross represents the normal reality of our everyday lives. Here we collect our experiences and relationships on a past-present-future "time line" of ongoing occurrences. Ordinary consciousness is limited to this material world of sequential events.

Non-ordinary consciousness puts us on "the vertical arm of the Cross," where we access soul memory. There we move in and out of different time periods without ever leaving the present moment's experience; in other words, we're in a timeless state. We may dip down and remember something from the past, or move upward and be shown something from the future, or we can even do both at once! But on the vertical dimension, whatever comes is always *experienced as happening now*.

In this way, we regress, turning back to re-experience and reclaim pieces of unfinished psychological work. Things that were repressed are released so we can truly know them and let them go. Or we might progress, moving forward to enter a greater reality or a "heaven world" out in the cosmos to learn some holistic truth, or simply to realize that we are bigger than we seem—which is healing in itself. In either case (whether moving back or forward), the body feels as if it's being transported to the other dimension; it feels like a *present-moment* experience.

Trance states, such as those produced by dreams, process hypnosis, meditation, and various kinds of breathwork,* provide this access to the various dimensions up and down the vertical arm. When we find ourselves "rising" into an expanded reality, and at the same time "falling" into a constricted one, we experience parallel universes or *simul-*

---

*Eupsychia's integrative breathwork is explained on page 53.

taneous realities. We leave the familiar mode of time known as "chronos" (the horizontal arm), and go into "kairos" time or soul time, which moves us along the vertical arm. And time becomes timeless.

Following are some examples of rising "above the horizon" on the vertical arm of the Cross, where spontaneous mystical experiences transcend ordinary time and space: In a dream, someone subjectively visits a friend who died and has come back into the dreamer's consciousness in an angelic state to disclose an important healing message. Or the dreamer is carried into the deceased person's heavenly abode to visit and begin to understand that way of being.

Several people during processes of inner work have experienced being revisited by children they lost, either through natural death, accident, or abortion. In one case, a child who was dead at birth told her grieving mother that she was exactly where she needed to be for her own soul's special needs, and that she was always there with her mother in the earthly dimension. Then she sent a symbolic image of herself for the mother to place in her heart so she could feel closer to her child. The image was a beautiful field of green grass where the child ran and played, and where the mother could join her. This type of inner experience can produce an instant resolution and healing.

When our consciousness drops us "below the horizon" in the vertical dimension of the inner worlds, deep psychological healings are possible. There we can clear painful issues left over from the past that have been repressed and untapped in our ordinary waking state. The important thing is to be able to access these old wounds experientially, to relive the actual repressed feelings. For example, a man might go all the way back to a pre-verbal time and relive traumatic sexual abuse, seeing real faces and other details, and having real biographical memories of the events that actually occurred.

But instead of being unconscious or terrified, he relives the event with the eyes of his soul wide open. Pent-up rage and tears are released, and his body naturally begins to make the movements it needs in order to be healed of the horror. He may sit up and worship, or take hold of the circumstances in such a way that this time he has power over the original powerless situation. He is "seeing double"— both as a wounded ego and as a soul who is above it all and was never damaged.

And this is how healing really happens. It's amazing to see a body do this holy work of redemption, which completely baffles the intellect! The intellect is too small to understand how healing really works; it's trying to think through it all without having to feel or forgive. And this simply doesn't work. An old adage says it all: "If you can't feel it, you can't heal it."

Continuing with the Cross symbolism: Besides representing "horizontal" events of ordinary-world time and the far less earthly experiences of "vertical" timelessness, the Cross image reminds us of balance. A balanced life requires some of both, and balance is the key here.

Too much ego work (the horizontal) becomes a deadly preoccupation with the past, or getting so caught up with every little detail that we lose sight of the bigger picture. Too much transcendence (vertical) makes us "spacy" and inefficient in ordinary life; it can take us into an irrelevant, time-wasting "spiritual by-pass."* Wholeness comes from living right at the point where horizontal and vertical meet. This is being centered, our natural healthy state.

The Body Knows

As shown in the preceding discussion about the vertical dimension of consciousness, the mind isn't the only place where our memories are stored. Besides the "thinking" kind of remembering, **CELLULAR MEMORY** is also available to us. This means that at the basic physical level of a single cell, our bodies hold onto experiences that later affect us.

Our bodies reflect our uncomfortable feelings by giving us spontaneous "startle" reactions, aches and pains, which will become disease if we ignore the earlier signals. And even when it doesn't come to physical impairment, cellular memory affects the way we perform routine tasks and react to times of stress and emotional trauma in our current situations.

Perhaps the earliest instance of cellular memory is **BIRTH EXPERIENCE IMPRINTING**, in which the actual conditions surrounding the birth process leave a record on the infant's psyche. This sets up a pattern or style of reaction to major life changes in the future. We usually are not conscious of these reactivities; we are simply at their mercy.

---

*This phrase was coined by psychologist John Welwood in the early 1970's.

[AUTHOR ANECDOTE FROM JACQUELYN] *I know this one really well, having been born two months premature. The "imprint" manifests in my life as an unrealistic approach to projects. Because I didn't have the opportunity of going through a normal 9-month gestation process, I tend to have a poor sense of time—inclined to plant seeds in the dead of winter! If something isn't all ready to go and looking successful, when only about 3/4 of the way into what would be its normal cycle, I can get very discouraged, thinking I've failed. Knowing more about natural timing earlier could have spared me a lot of pain.*

Another example of birth experience imprinting is in Caesarean section deliveries. It is typical for people who were born this way to unconsciously feel they've missed something. Because they were simply lifted out, they tend to have an exceptionally strong need to do things for themselves, and to "make it through," thereby compensating for the early incomplete experience.

And a third type of birth experience imprinting is when the mother has been anesthetized. It's as if the baby is knocked unconscious, and is never aware of a "conclusion." Later in life, each new pivotal situation is likely to cause a similar reaction, with the person feeling "foggy" and helplessly confused. It may bring on a literal grogginess in the face of choices, when appropriate action is called for.

An entirely different way of understanding cellular memory relates to dieting. Sometimes, after a certain amount of weight is lost, the loss suddenly stops. No matter how well the prescribed eating pattern is followed, no more weight comes off. This is called "plateauing." It happens when the dieter reaches a particular weight at which the body was comfortable at some point in the past. It remembers the weight level as a familiar condition, and chooses to stay at this plateau until jogged into action again by a new food pattern.

Memories of repressed childhood traumas, physical and emotional, are stored in cellular memory. Nothing we ever experience escapes the notice of our basic organisms. The great benefit of cellular memory is that it comes to the fore to take care of us when activated. The pitfall, of course, is that these old wounds, if not healed, can limit our freedom, and can even cause physical disease.

We can't rely on intellect alone to get us over a painful experience because the memories may be stuck—not in the mind, but—in the physical body. We heal by letting the body do its work in conjunction with Spirit, when the ego's intellect drops its tendency to be judgmental, and steps aside. *The body knows how to heal itself when we get out of its way.*

One method of doing this is a process called "integrative breathwork," a deep meditative inner journey set to music. By opening the psyche, which knows what each particular person needs, **BREATHWORK** offers an accelerated path to healing.

In a typical breathwork session, the body is first put into a light trance state, while the ego brain is allowed to "melt" through deep relaxation and guided imagery. Then wordless music begins and continues for about two hours.

The sounds progress from deep cultural drumming and chanting into melodies that bring up story lines from the subconscious. Later on, the music becomes emotionally or romantically evocative to open the heart. This is followed by "high" spiritual music, which has an uplifting effect, and can even activate a full-blown mystical experience. Finally, light-hearted and grounded "coming out" music provides the "breather" with a gentle return to everyday reality.

These sessions are free-associational journeys that activate the psyche and bring into conscious awareness any aspects of the past that must be remembered to be healed. And further, they let us imagine aspects of the future, as the human imagination—one of our most valuable soul powers —acts as a bridge between the conscious and unconscious minds, between our past and future lives. This imaginative cognition, together with inspiration and intuition, is a power of the Higher Mind.*

The science of vibration is essential to this healing process of breathwork, since the musical frequencies carry us along "memory lane," matching the blocked memories we need to access. In a non-ordinary state, the body spontaneously puts us into the physical positions necessary to re-create whatever it is that we need to relive in order to heal. *The body knows; the soul knows. Only the intellect can lie.*

Therapeutic methods like breathwork are successful when two elements are present—sacred space and surrender. We know that sacred space has been created when the atmosphere is *loving* and *safe* and *carries the conviction of its leaders* that Spirit is what's doing the work. Then an appropriate method (like an evocative musical journey) opens the psyche and brings the criteria for Spirit to flow, as our psyches must be *stirred* in order to open and release their contents. Surrendering to the process does the rest. People

*The powers of Higher Mind are explained in the chapter titled *Switching Priorities*, beginning on page 106.

having this experience need only to relax into it and *let it be* whatever it is. But, to attain the full benefits, they must also be willing to work with and integrate the material they've accessed.

Getting back to how our physical birth processes have programmed the templates of transformation into our psyches, what could be more logical? For, after all, to go from being a watery creature floating in a womb to an airy creature breathing the outside atmosphere is an obvious consciousness shift of dramatic proportions. Thus your biological birth process carries a key to understanding how you go through transformation at any stage of your life.*

EXERCISE: **Relating to Your Birth Pattern**

To get a clearer idea of how this works, stop now and reflect on the way you react when any of life's major shifts comes along. What messages do you give yourself about a big change when it first hits?

Write down your responses, and then ponder on the power of what you're noting. Now think about your emotional reactions: How do you feel when the old life starts falling away? Reflect on this feeling, and recall how far back it goes.

And finally, what is your mode of operation *when undergoing a transformation? Do you start, then stop? Procrastinate? Lose force and go passive? Push on through? Feel lost, unsure of which direction to take?*

Once you've done this bit of self-analysis, check with your

---

*For more information, refer to *Beyond the Brain* or *Adventures in Self-Discovery* by Stanislav Grof.

mother or others involved with your birth to learn about its pattern. Often the connection is very revealing.

The Heart Is the Bridge

"Heart" is a familiar word that means a lot more than the body's anatomical organ that pumps blood. **HEART** is also a metaphor for a sense of genuine and total clarity and feeling. It is that "place in consciousness" where someone experiences his or her true essence, and knows unconditional love. Just as the imagination is a bridge for the conscious-unconscious mind, the heart is the bridge between conscious and unconscious feelings and experiences.

It is through the heart that all our personal sorrows can rise up and meet the greater life with a deeper understanding and a more powerful Love. When our hearts are open we are filled with life; when closed, we are dead or deadened, and our lives seem non-relational and meaningless. And the heart never lies! It *cannot* lie. The heart knows only the truth of what we really feel at any moment, no matter how much the intellect may try to talk us out of it.

The new-world-view way of looking at life differently requires the ability to "see" from the heart, rather than the intellect. While the intellect exists to analyze, define, and categorize information, the heart simply loves. In fact, it can be safely said that the intellect divides, and the heart unites.

When we are seeing through the heart's love, we can include the mind with love, and break loose from the "trap of dualism" that blocks healing. **DUALISM** means that the world is made up of pairs of opposites—which is simply *a fact* on this planet Earth. We tend to turn this fact into a restrictive either/or kind of thinking, however, which looks at all matters as *conflicting opposites*, rather than *harmonious polarities*; for example, masculine/feminine, active/passive, past/future, shadow/light, ego/soul.

Everything has its opposite precisely because this polarity is what allows for creative action. And all the opposites within us are "lovers" seeking to unite. But to know true union, we must first experience both sides of each pair separately.

Just as we must come to know the ego and the soul, we must also know the shadow and the light in every situation. Then we can drop any judgment of either side, recognize that any form of "two-ness" is the actual function of Creativity itself, a "fire by friction" that produces a third and greater thing.

We can learn to make each opposition within us *complementary* rather than conflictual by honoring the friction of the opposites as having a sacred function.

While the pairing of opposites is natural, when too much energy goes into an "either/or" mentality, we can become fixated into some kind of fanaticism or one-sidedness, and we lose our balance. Then like a pendulum stretched all the way to one side, we carry too much tension too far away from center. And think how a pendulum must feel pulled to this extreme, and held there! Dualism can be a trap that prevents the kind of creativity required of the new breed of healers or anyone else on a soul-centered path of awakening.

To remain broad-minded and uninvested in any biased

outcome is a high attainment, a form of spiritual integrity. We must not let the old judgmental ways keep us from being in the center of ourselves, the only place where ego and soul can merge, the only place where the Self can walk in. Since the heart allows no imbalance, both sides of any apparent duality must be experienced and accepted if we are ever to know fulfillment.

It is only through the gateway of the open heart that we can enter into the field of love and the unity consciousness that feeds our hungry souls. We master the tests of duality through acceptance and forgiveness, which come from understanding both sides of any opposition. Paradoxically, our complete acceptance of *both* the dark *and* the light is what actually transforms dualism. For once we recognize that the "opposing poles" are really all one thing, then we see unity, the *one* that both really are. And so unity replaces dualism.*

When you are coming from the heart, you'll notice you are above judgment, and can see the big picture. Think of a time recently when you had a "heart to heart" talk with a friend. Remember how it felt? In the heart, we have no ax to grind, no position to defend.

From this perspective, we understand how both the negative and positive sides of ourselves are valid and purposeful. Then we can start to let go, forgive, and move on to a new way of being, clear of the old pattern or situation. This is the process of death/rebirth; we *dis*identify from one set of conditions, and *re*identify at a higher level.

*Dualism is discussed earlier in Part 1, under *The Challenge Ahead*, page 22.

[AUTHOR ANECDOTE FROM MARY] *During one breathwork session, I'd drifted into a familiar theme, the proverbial "mother-daughter conflict." But instead of seeing it from my usual daughter's viewpoint, I suddenly "got a flash" of my mother's. How awful to bring someone into the world who later seems to be in constant conflict. I felt her trying her best, and not knowing what had gone wrong. With an open heart came deeper understanding. Though our relationship may never be perfect, the compassion pouring through me that day forever changed the way I look at it.*

It has been said that a heart breaks open so wisdom can flow in. The mystery of the Heart contains a web of meaning to be unraveled. An open heart gives insight for dealing with the two opposite poles of dualism, or "the tension of the opposites," which leads to bliss.* Here's another example: The feeling of complete devastation from the loss of a loved one who is dying can be held steady with a simultaneous feeling of radiating joy for this person's release from suffering.

Pleasure and pain are one in the heart's bliss. Denying neither the one nor the other—*this* is the activity of the Heart. The "divine tension" of the expanding and contracting Heart keeps us in touch with our whole nature, our joys and our sorrows all mixed up together. Neither one is sought after or wallowed in, nor despised or ignored; the two become a third and higher thing. This is the emotional freedom of bliss!

---

*The tension-of-the-opposites concept is discussed further under *Living from Center*, page 103.

In summary, an open heart holds the key to healing. It is where the ego and the soul meet, the bridge between dualism and unification. It is through the melting of our dualistic attitude—all our one-sided judgments and opinions —that we are released from our separatist thinking and self-ish pursuits. Then we can live in the conscious state of the open Heart, capable of unifying our personal and collective realities.

Anytime we get stuck in our minds, trying to figure out things intellectually, or trying to detach from and rise above a condition, the Heart can remind us to let ourselves feel it *thoroughly*, to complete it with full understanding before we walk away. And understanding can come only when we have felt something all the way through. The essentials of anything can be known *only* in the heart. For, paraphrasing the Agni Yoga teachings: Until we can see with the eyes of the Heart, listen to the roar of the world through the ears of the Heart, and peer into the future with the comprehension of the Heart, we can never know a thing, nor will we ever be whole. The Heart unites us all, regardless of our differences, in this common understanding, and brings compassion to our troubled world.

The Heart cannot be known intellectually; it must be experienced. Perhaps doing this exercise will help bring this concept home to you.

Exercise: **Opening Your Heart**

Allow yourself to reflect on a personal problem you are having. See it clearly in your mind. . . . Experience the feeling in your body that this problem gives you . . . the emotion . . . the pain. . . . Let it come on up. . . .

Gently breathe into the area around your heart, as you let go of any tightness or anxiety that has come up. . . . Feel yourself letting go as your body relaxes. . . . If you feel any emotion rocking around, breathe quietly in and out for as long as you need to, letting your heart-space become more and more clear of any tension or imbalance. . . . Just breathe. . . . And relax. . . .

At this point, music can deepen the experience—some lovely wordless heartfelt music.

Now look back at the scene with the person or people you are having the struggle with, as if you are looking down from above it. See the other or others, the whole scene more clearly with your Heart wide open. . . . Feel what the others are going through . . . the hurt . . . the disappointment . . . the fear. . . . Now see yourself and feel into yourself as well. . . . Take on all of it, as much as you can, with open-hearted compassion. . . .

Find the meaning and sacred purpose of this entire event. . . . And send down Love and Light to all concerned. . . . Surrender your mind into Love. . . . Expand your Heart into true acceptance and forgiveness. . . . Embrace the wound in the Light of Understanding and Compassion. . . . And love your Self as much as you can from wherever you are with this situation. . . .

Then gradually let the scene fade, and slowly come back to this reality. Take some time to reflect on what just happened, and feel whatever else is going on inside your body right now. . . . You may want to write or draw for a while, or discuss this experience with a trusted friend.

Our Many Selves

Though we will eventually know ourselves better—each of us as one unified whole Self—for now, most are somewhat fragmented. We have within us many selves, all living in the same body/mind, sometimes at war, and sometimes fully conscious and cooperative. Surely you have realized that sometimes one part of you wants one thing, while another wants the opposite. Or a part of you chooses to grow, while another one resists. Then a third voice in your head may be fussing at you because you can't make a decision! Sometimes these many selves function just like a committee. And you know how dysfunctional a committee can be when trying to arrive at a consensus!

These different selves relate to the various approaches we use in dealing with life. And because we are spiritual beings inhabiting human bodies, each of these ''selves'' has an important sacred function in our awakening. They can be thought of as characters that play vital and divine roles in our world drama. If we understand their nature, and honor them each for exactly what they represent, they will bring us their gifts—even those selves who seem to be negative.

For our healing and fulfillment as human souls, it is up to us to learn to coordinate these differing aspects of our Personhood. And hopefully, at some point in doing our inner work, we will gain enough Self-awareness to willfully employ them when needed, under the direction of our core Identity, the true Self.

This Self functions like the nucleus of a cell, an embodied, soul-centered Personality, the one who is back there behind all our human endeavors. For the Self is both the *originator* and the *completer* of all our life's experiences. First it sets up the circumstances as individually needed, and then it moves into our bodies, minds, and hearts, taking on life's conditions. When we really "get it" that we are spiritual beings in human form, our lives acquire a sacred purpose that brings with it a healing factor and significant meaning. As Carl Jung so beautifully expresses this:

> "If one knows that one has been singled out by divine choice and intention from the beginning of the world, then one feels lifted beyond the transitoriness and meaninglessness of ordinary human existence, and transported to a new state of dignity and importance, like one who has a part in the divine world drama."
>
> —*Answer to Job*

As a guide to your transformative work, this chapter describes each of the many "selves" we all must necessarily employ. You'll read about their functions—so you can recognize them when they come into play—plus some suggestions on how to intentionally put each of them to good use. For people on the path of transformation find that their utilization of these blessed human/divine "selves" has everything to do with how they heal and become integrated individuals. When we call on these entities, we are tapping into our inner powers of Being.

You will recognize these many selves, since you already know them well. For they have always been with you, and always will be, until the end of Time.

EGO

Let's begin with the most familiar self—who, by the way, gets quite a bad press: the ego. We all know we react negatively to people who are being egotistical, ego-invested, or "egoed out"! This character is the executor of our personal identity, the ruler of our conscious waking life. It is the part of us who separates us off so we can differentiate from other souls in human form. The "bad press" arises from the ego's purpose—taking care of you and only you in this material world, no matter what! This means it can even harm another on your behalf if you are unconscious of its ways. The human ego is the "lord of materialism" and knows the ways of the world from aeons of experience here. Remember the cave man who would clobber a neighbor with a club in order to confiscate his woman or his meat?

When aligned with your true Self, however, your ego is your very best friend, and a sacred aspect of your divine nature. Though we are both individuals and parts of a collective one Humanity, the ego is designed to serve the personal self, making certain our *individual* needs are met.

We all have basic human needs for food, safety, pleasure, nurturing, relationship, self-esteem, personal strength, and love. If we become too needy in any of these areas of our lives, the ego gets nervous and behaves badly. We become too ego-invested, and "want what we want when we want it," often at some other poor person's expense.

Your ego is not the least concerned whether your needs are good for the whole. Our egos are looking out for each of us, individually. For without meeting our own basic human needs, we become imbalanced and miserable, and can even get sick and die. Therefore, to our egos, meeting our personal needs is a life-and-death matter.

THE EGO'S SACRED FUNCTION

Your ego creates an "ego ideal," or social self, worthy of the admiration of others, a positive self image for you to shine through. It invents the face you wear for others to see and relate to. These social selves of ours came into being when we were young, in order to get the "ego strokes" that made up our positive self-images. Therefore, the ego looks different in different societies, as it puts on whatever costume fits the cultural ideal.

The ego also keeps us safe from ever becoming overwhelmed by the abstract contents of our unconscious processes, or by life in general. So the ego is about limitation; it decides which boundaries we must live within and call "reality." Whatever it cannot accept as legitimate gets thrown out, discounted, or labeled as wrong, dangerous or even unreal. When some concept or situation is only partly accepted by the ego, we feel a terrible upset within the psyche—nightmares, irrational fears, etc.—until the material being processed is either made acceptable or discarded.

In this way, our egos try to keep us from disintegrating when anything that is "too much" hits our psyches. When we become reactive to anything, this is the ego's way of showing us something doesn't feel right, or is an outright threat to us. It can even become overly protective or pre-occupied with meeting some unmet need, to the point of blocking our growth into new, expanded ways of being.

When the ego is gratified, it turns to higher things: It functions in alignment with the soul, having presence, potency, and a strong sense of earthly wisdom. It will eventually disappear into a soul-centered personality, which explains why spiritually-advanced people often appear to be almost egoless. Just the same, never forget that even saints and gurus have egos; for without them, they could not function on the Earth plane.

There is a saying in transformational psychology: ''Ego integration must precede ego transcendence.'' In other words, we must *have* an ego before we can move beyond it. People with no ego strength live in back wards of mental hospitals, unable to handle the simplest tasks. Therefore, it's up to each of us to develop a healthy, emotionally balanced and realistic ego, to gain a positive self-image, grounded in this material world. Until we learn to meet our basic needs in a healthy fashion, we have no foundation on which our true and balanced Self, the soul, can stand.

No one but you can ever meet your basic needs, no matter how hard they try. This is something we must always be willing to do for ourselves, and to let go of the unrealistic notion that anyone else is ever responsible for our feelings or our well-being. Otherwise, we become ''codependent,'' leaning on others to meet our needs for us, and that creates dysfunctional, unhappy relationships.

Think how it feels whenever people pull on you to give them their emotional well-being, or indeed, their very lives! Anytime we're made to feel guilty or coerced into an unhealthy bonding like this, we feel it as the squeamish bodily sensation of being smothered. We make excuses to get away from the person, or hear ourselves saying, "I need some space." So obviously, we don't want to come across that way ourselves!

To help you deal with this kind of neediness in yourself, following is an exercise for use at any time you are having that "clutched" feeling of craving something or someone you've just *got to have*. The craving might be for sweets, another person to make you feel secure, a pleasurable "high," a sexual turn-on, or some kind of status symbol or reward to raise your self-esteem.

EXERCISE: **Activating Your Healthy Ego**

When obsessing about a need for anything outside yourself to make you feel whole, have a little talk with your ego. Remember: *You* are *not* your ego; your ego is something you *have*. Remind yourself that you are a spiritual being, a Self much greater than your ego.

Noticing this "needy attack" is half the battle, and remembering that you are not your conditions is even more of the battle won. For when we can make something conscious we gain its power; but anything left unconscious has power over us.

Activate your imagination to see your ego as an inner character. Once it appears, note what costume it's wearing. Then see it aligning with your highest Self, willing and ready to be drafted into an important assignment. Calling on your creative imagination carries you even further toward the self-mastery you seek. For now you—as your greater Self—are in charge.

Remember that you always have a choice: You can either go for the object of craving unconsciously—eating those 14 cookies, or calling that unresponsive lover for the hundredth time—knowing you may regret it later; or you can be conscious about it.

Ask your ego what it is yearning for, so you can find a way to meet the need in a positive manner. Separate the need *from the* object *of the craving. While the need may be valid, you may be going after the wrong thing for its true gratification.*

For example, let's say you are feeling empty, useless. Instead of "filling up" on food, try another way to satisfy the emptiness. Ask yourself what non-caloric activity thoroughly pleases you— perhaps painting pictures, photographing beautiful artifacts, reading books, taking walks in nature, calling a friend. Be creative! Decide on something that is healthy and life-giving, that doesn't harm yourself or anyone else.

Then treat yourself to this pleasure. Bask in it, to become full again.

And one more thing: If you hear any negative "self-talk" going on in your head about how miserable or unlovable you are, stop it! Instead of replaying these old tapes, just change the subject.

Take a moment to thank yourself for allowing you this time for the healthful diversion you deserve. Then thank your ego for its part in bringing you to this corrective action.

The important thing in this exercise is to always be blatantly honest with yourself about what you truly need—just learning to claim it without shame, without feeling like a victim of anything or anyone.

Denying our truth of the moment and attempting to repress our needs never gets us where we want to be. Yet, even though they come up to tempt us, we don't ever have to act on personal needs that harm us or others.

It takes practice to find positive substitutes for those wrong turns we make when "looking for love in all the wrong places" (which never truly gratify us at all). Make a pact with yourself that you're worth the time and trouble it takes to develop such healthy substitutions—which, once learned, can rapidly change your life. Though it is very hard to step out of old ruts, we must learn, for as the Agni Yoga teachings state so poignantly:

> "It is dreadful when [people] approach new conditions with their old habits. Just as it is impossible to open a present-day lock with a medieval key, likewise it is impossible for [people] with old habits to unlock the door to the future."

SHADOW

This is an unwanted self who is repressed and unavailable to consciousness unless some deep inner work brings it to the surface. We actually despise this part of us. Just as your ego is in charge of your conscious life, your shadow is the holder of your unconscious aspects and processes.

Your shadow is made up of all those disowned traits you never want to have, and certainly if you do have them, you hope they will never show. It is the exact opposite of your ideal. For example, if you pride yourself on being a moral upright citizen, your shadow is that urge you get to be an untamed rogue who lusts after some ghastly forbidden vice. Or if your ideal image is someone of dignified repose, your shadow is the wild-eyed hysteric or "rage-aholic" who bursts out when you've had enough of being calm; it stomps and screams to get its point across, saying things you later regret. If you are sexually repressed, your shadow may be a vamp or one who secretly enjoys pornography. If you are successful and balanced economically, your shadow is a spendthrift or a miser. When not owned, your negative side acts out "behind your back," which means these despised behaviors sometimes come out while you're pretending they don't exist.

All our personality traits and emotions that did not fit in with our ego ideal or our family's moral code got repressed very early in life and built up into our shadow. To please others and to be loved, we had to hide these parts of our natural selves—usually feelings pertaining to sexuality or the natural expressions of anger, fear, weakness, or disagreement with some authority figure. And besides these "negatives," we also have talents and unrealized, untapped potential that are hidden in our shadow as well.

The shadow lives in our "emotional body," the carrier of exaggerated, ill-formulated, immature feelings. It is slippery and hard to catch hold of in the light of day because we've so buried it. Your shadow is your "dark side"—made up of little personalities living in your unconscious mind who represent these repressed urges all mixed up with one another. Since they are not available for reality testing (because you've denied they even exist), and are not conscious at all, sexual desire may be lumped in with rage and shame, for example, though these three feelings don't even belong together! Or natural urges toward leadership may be fused alongside boisterous, boastful expressions that turn people off—not a bit like true leadership. All these kinds of repressed emotionally charged energies make up the human shadow.

But psychic or emotional energy has no place to go

when repressed. So, as if they're in a pressure cooker, these unexpressed urges build up inside us, just waiting for a chance for release. Standing at the threshold between our conscious and unconscious minds, our shadow reflects back whatever's being hidden or denied. And until we make this unloved part of ourselves conscious, it can burst out with no warning as an explosion of emotionalism or in some other obnoxious and humiliating manner. Grounded in fear, defensiveness, drama, immaturity, and competitiveness, our shadows can destroy us and our relationships if not made conscious.

THE SHADOW'S SACRED FUNCTIONS

The shadow has three sacred functions: (1) It will not allow us to deny any parts of ourselves or any unfinished psychological business we're avoiding. (2) It carries our passions. So when accepted and allowed to integrate, the shadow brings us a greater sense of aliveness. (3) It gives us compassion. Once we can own our shadows, we can be more understanding of others when we see them acting out of *their* dark sides. We become non-judgmental and forgiving, safe listeners for others to tell their darkest secrets to— which can be very healing for them.

To elaborate on these three sacred functions, first: The shadow serves as a constant reminder of any unintegrated emotional material we are hoping to skip over and sneak past. And it will go to any ends to get our attention, including embarrassing us greatly! By revealing those feelings we hate to admit about ourselves, the shadow forces us to grow beyond them, leading us toward our wholeness.

This can be explained by the ancient concept of a great

psychological law that keeps us from getting too one-sided. This law, called **ENANTIODROMIA**, says that all extremes eventually turn to their polar opposites. This concept comes into play whenever we become so obsessed with one side of a polarity that we don't even acknowledge the other. Eventually, we have to face the exact opposite, the side we've been denying in ourselves. Psyche sees that we know enough about the one, so presents inner messages or outer life experiences that force us to recognize the side of the polarity that we find so unpleasant. Our psyche is invested in *completion*, not perfection!

Here's an example you might be familiar with: A married couple who are always smiling and claim they never have any reason to argue. At some point, they can no longer continue their forced niceness. This often plays out when both partners explode, letting out all their previously denied resentments; and the result is a bitter divorce or a hideous custody battle.

The second function: Since the shadow is the holder of our human passions, developing a healthy conscious relationship with it makes us much more alive, interesting, and intensely involved with life—which is far more fulfilling than living a lukewarm existence.

And third: Our shadow brings us compassion—and also credibility—when we own it. Perhaps you can now see what a sacred character it truly is! Having learned from the pain of dealing with our own shadow issues, we become more human. So this third gift from the shadow is the chance to ''get real'' by taking responsibility for our part in any relationship dysfunction, and thereby improving relations all around. Others trust us and want to be with us when they sense that we'll claim our own "stuff" rather than blaming them whenever a disagreement occurs.

Everyone has a shadow! When we recognize and take responsibility for our shadows by owning them—out loud with no shame—our lives become more integrated; the extremes begin to move toward center, and we learn to live with the "tension of the contraries" inside us—never all right, never all wrong, all bad or all good—just *human*, and absolutely okay with who we are.

When we choose to awaken and enter the spiritual path, the shadow is the first of our many selves we encounter. This explains why we often look worse instead of better, once we decide to wake up. The shadow will eventually bring out of denial all our unconscious ways. And what a gift! Paradoxically, the more we own this self, the less we see of it.*

EXERCISE: **Healing Your Shadow**

Take a deep breath and settle down for some inner work. Begin reflecting on what you just read about your shadow self. Now imagine your shadow living right under the floor, awaiting your recognition. Listen carefully, as your shadow moves around down there.

Pay close attention . . . watch a trap door starting to open, then your shadow sticking out its head to give you a glimpse. What comes? Notice your shadow emerging and coming fully into view.

Once you can see all of your shadow, take in its expression and

---

*The concept of shadow is discussed further throughout the next chapter, *The Importance of Shadow Work.*

''body language.'' Notice how its presence makes you feel. Try to talk with your shadow, and love it as much as you can. If this is difficult, just be with whatever you're feeling without judging it.

When you've reached a point of closure for now, see your shadow returning to the trap door, and on down to its place below. Then write down what this experience has meant to you, or do some drawing to capture it.

Practice this exercise as often as you can. Learn to dialogue with your shadow so that eventually it becomes a real person who can travel consciously with you through your days and nights. Let it know that you will take care of its needs the best you can, but also that you plan to stay in charge of your life!

By using your creative imagination, you can make this self a real and valuable friend, and in its own way, a wise teacher. But don't ever forget: *The shadow has shadow nature!* And it always will. Like an immature child, it will always behave as untamed, ill formed and hard to love.

INNER CHILD

The archetypal Child within you is the Soul, who never experiences the pain inflicted upon many a human child in this troubled world of ours. This Child within is devoid of human experience. Its pure innocence is not a safe reality for ordinary human beings, for it cannot tell the difference between something safe and something that will expose it to danger.

During abuse or neglect, the soul leaves the body and soars into the heaven worlds where it is at Home. And there, for the suffering child, it becomes the Magical Child, who will make up whatever reality or ''special friend'' it chooses, to comfort itself. Wounded children remind us of this sacred gift of a magical life with their non-attachment to ordinary reality. We actually experience this Divine Child as the wounded one so common in the field of addictions recovery.

Though you may be familiar with the biographical wounded child we can become after birth, which is part of the ego, don't confuse it with the Divine Child archetype who lives within us. The Divine Child is playful, innocent, and always willing to enter into new experiences, taking with it a loving spontaneity. When it doesn't find delight, it recedes. Or it carries us elsewhere so we can know the holy pleasure of innocence and pure joy. The Divine Child is never born, never wounded, and never dies.

THE INNER CHILD'S SACRED FUNCTION

Wide-eyed and spirit-filled, this inner Child lives to maintain our innocence for us—no matter what. It can always bring us to a fresh place, seeing things anew with wonder. Anytime we get too bogged down with life's predicaments, become too "weighted," too intellectual, or start to take ourselves too seriously, it can come in and remind us of our sacred Innocence. This self urges us to remember to see and feel things freshly, spontaneously, and with awe. Often we experience this child inwardly as a playful cherub.

EXERCISE: **Connecting with Your Inner Child**

If you have trouble knowing how to play, or if you counsel clients who are taking themselves too seriously, bringing this inner archetype to life will help to lighten the heaviness that comes from being overrun with responsibil-ity. This example is given as if you were working with a client; after familiarizing yourself with it, you can tailor the steps for your own personal use. Begin guiding the process by saying:

Close your eyes and imagine the innocent Child who lives within you. . . . See it clearly now, and let it show you something hidden, some happy surprise. . . . (Long pause.)

Now describe out loud what you are experiencing. . . .

After listening to the client's description, continue with the imagery in a manner that fits this particular person's needs. For example: *Let your inner Child hand you a symbol to remind you of its presence. Place the symbol in your heart, for you to carry it there always. Notice how you feel having this special gift living in your heart.*

Or—a variation: *Bring your Inner Child into your heart and know that it lives there always. Know that this Divine Child can be communicated with, or "brought to life" when needed. The only requirement is your willingness to practice spontaneity or playful-ness, or enter into some aspect of your life with the freshness a child would bring to the situation.*

Help the client bring this imagery to an appropriate closure. For example: *As you get ready to open your eyes and fully return to this ordinary reality, know that your inner child will be consciously with you from now on.*

A note about interpreting symbols: Symbols that come to us during inner work are clues as to what our psyches are trying to tell us. We should pay attention and try to under-stand what the symbolism means. A number of books are available that outline the universal implications of certain specific symbols, and these may be helpful. The most important part of any symbol analysis, however, is to trust one's own inner teacher. So if you do consult some kind of reference material, note only those meanings that ring true for you. For your personal interpretations always carry more weight than any "outside authority." Also be careful not to impose your interpretations on someone else's symbols.

HIGHER SELF

This Self is the Divine Ideal of every human being—our core nature or root-consciousness, which draws Its energy from the Creator or God-force. It is your "Transpersonal" Self who lives "in the world but not of it." Remember, **TRANSPERSONAL** means both *going through* and *moving beyond*. Your Higher Self can be here as your fully blossomed Self, or it can rise above it all and stay in the heaven worlds, containing both personal and universal consciousness. This divine/human Self never gets identified with its conditions nor loses its Identity. It knows it is of God!

The Higher Self is also known as the Soul-in-incarnation, a mediator between earth life and divine life. It has the highest attributes we humans are capable of, representing our greatest ideals. When activated in our lives, we experience ourselves as being wise, calm, centered, compassionate, and lighthearted—with a deep sense of well-being. When completely merged with this highest Self, we have no unmet needs. You could even say that for the moment we are enlightened. Rarely, though, is anyone constantly anchored in this Self. Jesus was, when "Christed"; and the Buddha, when he realized "Buddha nature." Though most of us are lucky to have even a few moments of this type of exalted consciousness, we must strive to make this Self our reality. For, as Saint Paul noted: This Christ consciousness is our hope and our glory.

THE HIGHER SELF'S SACRED FUNCTION

Acting as our Blueprint, our Divine Ideal, this Self is always calling us to our highest expression by bringing on a "divine discontent" anytime we get off the mark. Always moving us to be like our inner God-image, the Higher Self is our guy-wire Home. It will never let us rest until we fully grow into who we were intended to be.

The Higher Self's function is to remind us of our greatest potential whenever we get stuck in the human condition—to remember our origins, that we are sons and daughters of God. The Higher Self sends us its qualities of creative imagination, inspiration, and awesome revelations, just so we can recall that we have a sacred purpose for being here in this world.

It is *by*, *through* and *as* this Self that we eventually evolve into our completion. In the meantime, It brings us all the lessons we need—actually setting them up, in fact—and carries us through whatever we must undergo in order to become likened to this Ideal. And so the Higher Self guides you through all the challenges necessary to fulfill your mission here—to become your fully realized divine/human Self. Unfortunately, we usually do not remember this great Truth until some tragedy forces us to rise to our highest expression. But eventually humankind will learn to live as this One who comes straight from the heaven worlds, right here in this world!

Exercise: **Aligning with Your Higher Self**

To heal and become whole, we must practice aligning with our Higher Self, first by *making it real*. This means we must know that we have a Higher Self living inside our very own minds and hearts. We make it legitimate by believing in it, not simply as a figment of our fancy, but knowing it as a real live Entity—the You that you were designed to be. The Higher Self is our wholeness pattern.

Have you realized yet that *you* are the only one who can give *your* meaning to anything—even to your decision about God's identity? Stop and reflect on this, and you will see how true it is. You can practice this "making it real" by following the steps below.

Sit in repose, bringing your highest Ideal Self into your mind; see it as your Divine Ideal image—making this image real by your intention to do so.

Now ask your Higher Self to relate to you, and see what happens in your inner life.

When the relationship between the two of you feels right, have your Higher Self send you an object to represent It, and to help you remember in the future who you are at your divine Core. Always and already, you *are this Self.*

Let this concept and image sink into your consciousness; anchor it as the way you'd like to live all the time—*as both that One who is fully in this world, and simultaneously that One who is beyond it, untouched by our human trials. This is how you learn to live where doubt can no longer reach you; you come* fully *into your Self.*

If you are a counselor, you will sometimes have clients who are so filled with doubt and low self-esteem that they'll tell you they don't even believe they have a Higher Self. Whenever this happens, you can say, "Well, *if you did* have a Higher Self, what would It say right now about this current predicament you're in?" Without fail, the client will say something like, "It would tell me to get out of this mess right now—to just leave!" Or, "Oh, my wiser part knows that I should take this job." And with such conviction! Then, of course, you can point out the amazing fact that the client does indeed have a wise Self within. For, "Listen to who just spoke!"

All we can ever do is ask, and Higher Self is there. When we are willing to rise to the Call, we always get a response. Our willingness is the key.

OBSERVER SELF

The Observer Self is your Higher Self's mind—its way of "thinking." It is also known as your inner Masculine Principle, because of its quality of logical detachment. The Observer is the "Fair Witness" consciousness the Buddhists speak of, keyed to your greater life, which is unfolding on a larger canvas. And it never leaves you, though you may be unconscious of it most of the time—until you recognize it and make it a welcome part of your life.

When activated, we can see the overview, and think clearly, beyond all contradictions. This is the inner knower. And we can call on it anytime we feel we are getting hooked in some aspect of life and losing our objectivity. Jung described the clarity of observer consciousness like this:

"What, on a lower level, had led to the wildest conflicts and to panicky outbursts of emotion, now looks like a storm in the valley seen from the mountain top. This does not mean that the storm is robbed of its reality, but instead of being in it, one is above it.''

—*Alchemical Studies*

THE OBSERVER SELF'S SACRED FUNCTION

The Observer Self is our awakener—the one who nudges us gently every time we "fall asleep at the wheel," when we're acting against our own best interests without realizing it. For example, imagine yourself in the middle of a typical family battle. You're about to scream at your daughter, determined to enforce some old rule, when suddenly the "light bulb comes on." You remember she's just growing up. Now—with conscious awareness—you can stick to the unbending stance you've used since she was a child, or you can practice treating her like an adult. You always have the choice.

This is how the Observer "speaks," with those "Ahas!" that come out of the blue. It never preaches or judges us; it just reveals the truth in instant realizations. It is our wake-up call that functions like a snooze alarm, which won't let us rest in any sleep state for very long. Observer consciousness holds "the bird's eye view," never falling into unconscious situations that cause us to be blinded by limitation. Observer calls us to participate consciously in our own creation, moment by moment. And once we are "on the path," it will never let us rest in any kind of unreality.

So your Observer Self keeps you awake and at the midpoint, and helps you avoid the extremes, for it's through the Middle Way that we find peace of mind. All the great spiritual paths lead to this kind of balanced living. Once Observer becomes your constant conscious companion, you will be aware that your self-image is changing and expanding. You will see that *how* you see a thing determines the *what* of it. And this is very self-empowering—to know that we can always change our minds, whenever we feel trapped in some unrealistic or unfulfilled way of being.

EXERCISE: **Calling Out Your Observer Self***

Anytime you feel you've gotten caught up in an untruth or unhealthy activity, and can no longer ''see the forest for the trees,'' stop and enact the magic formula outlined below.

First, calm down. Sit still, take a deep breath, and remind yourself that Observer can help. Now try to rise above the whole scenario, and observe it ''from above.'' See it all clearly—what is really going on, why, and how. Work out all the details, as if you were a disinterested party, merely reporting on it.

Next focus on what you spiritually intend. Then use your creative imagination to envision a desired outcome, and mentally change your direction to achieve it.

Later on, during the ordinary course of your routine activities, take this new direction, giving it full manifestation in your life. This is putting into action the powers of Sincerity and Willingness. And once you've done this, the rest is Higher Power's part.

---

*Another exercise for working with the Observer Self is given in the next chapter, page 101.

INNER BELOVED

This aspect of our inner Self represents the spiritual contra-sexual counterpart or ideal that lives inside the heart of each of us. It is the sacred "Beloved of the Soul," which is spoken of by the Sufi tradition and written about in many a poet's intense yearning for true love. This is the inner side that remained subjective and has never taken earthly form; that is, the divine "Other"—the one you lack in your outer expression, your "missing part."

Our hunger to merge with divine Love continually propels us forward to achieve union and completion, forever moving toward the expression of our Ideal. This marriage of the inner Soul with the outer human self or personality, brings our "spirit/matter" state into wholeness. When the two marry in our subjective life, we become androgynous, meaning that we now have within our own nature a balance of masculine and feminine energies, all we ever need to be fulfilled. We walk the earth as an embodied Soul.

THE INNER BELOVED'S SACRED FUNCTION

This archetypal inner Partner brings us the passionate inspiration and creativity we feel anytime we fall in love. The Beloved keeps "the dream" alive. If we are truly honest with ourselves, isn't this the ideal state we'd prefer to live in always? But this "in-loveness" state, remember, cannot be attached to a specific person or form. That would be an illusion, or half-truth. Living "in Love" and passionately inspired is *a state of consciousness only*, one available to us all, even when we have no partner of any kind in the outer world.

When we do try to attach this inner Ideal Other onto any one poor unsuspecting human being, we are doing that person a disfavor; and we're likely to get all caught up in a relationship with someone who can never live up to our ideal. This can create a tragic love affair, or at the very least, an immature, unconscious relationship. We can never make a mere mortal into a god, or expect Perfect Love from any one among us—at least not at this stage of our evolution. We *can* have those precious moments when a lover or mate fulfills this strong archetypal desire. But we should never cling to these moments, only cherish them and let them go.

This inner Partner provides the sacred function of moving us toward our *own* completion, which does not depend on anyone else being in our lives to outwardly gratify us. Not that we don't prefer (and deserve) some "other" to celebrate our unique expression with—this is only too human, and a normal part of nearly anyone's growth here in this world. But we are not to confuse the inner Beloved with any regular person; the Beloved is *all* the lovers in the world we could ever dream of, all put together. We've made him or her into our *own* ideal. And this inner Ideal never has to take on a form. Therefore, it can remain as "perfect" and "pure" as our heart's desire.

The inner Beloved brings a sense of the sacred mystery of "Holy Matrimony" into our lives as a *felt* experience. But only if we learn to go within and commune with Him or Her from the subjective worlds. Then occasionally here and there, with any one lover or partner in life, Its divine qualities will shine through. And for a moment, we are in ecstasy —and transformed.

In the old days, these inner Lovers were known as "daimons" who ignite our creativity into a blazing fire of inspiration for the world, making us feel whole. (Dante's Beatrice is a fine example.) And this, our wholeness, is the true spiritual gift that we give back to the world for giving us life. This is our service—our true calling—to come fully into our Self.

Inner Lovers are a fact within the psychic realms. We *do* have "split-aparts" who adore us and guide us from within. But these inner Beloveds are just this: a psychospiritual evolutionary function that can be known only from within. Much glamor and illusion are built up around this particular archetype. Remember, your Beloved is the other half of *you, the part who never incarnated, but whispers to you from within.* So, quite naturally, we continually seek some reminder of this divine "Other" in our outer world.

When the archetypal Beloved is constellated within our psyches, we come to know a balance between the Masculine and Feminine poles within us. Carl Jung believed this marriage of the Masculine and Feminine Principles is our final stage of becoming whole. In his words:

> "In communing with himself he finds not deadly boredom and melancholy but an inner partner, more than that, a relationship that seems like the happiness of a secret love, or like a hidden springtime, when the green seed sprouts from the barren earth, holding out the promise of future harvests."
> —*Collected Works*

Exercise: **Constellating Your Inner Beloved**

Take some time to sit for a while, and reflect on all those men or women you've been in love with in your life. Bring to your conscious awareness the qualities they possess that caused you to have that "in love" feeling . . . that "look" in their eyes, the fragrance when present, the tones of voice, their posture or gait, those unique traits that made each of them so special . . .

Now—as if by magic—allow your imagination to make all these lovers into One Person who now lives inside of you. See Who emerges from within. Recall how this "Other" has been with you, and all the ways He or She has always been there, disguised as various voices or images in your dreams or that One you've always carried in your mind and heart.

Allow the Beloved to speak to you from within. Listen carefully in the silence of your own heart. When you hear the message, just revel in your Beloved's presence for a while. Then capture your feelings on paper somehow, and cherish this special time of communing with your inner Partner.

INNER HEALER

This is the self who comes to us like a benevolent Angel, providing the additional energy, strength, or hope we sometimes need to get beyond some aspect of ill health that is causing us to feel overcome.

Healing is the judicious use of our human energy system applied with love *and* scientific knowledge. To heal ourselves of any physical issue, it is important today to remember that we are in a transition period between med-

ical systems that are transforming. An "integrative approach" is therefore recommended—utilizing both medical
knowledge based on the most modern empirical research,
and alternative systems of healing. Perhaps not yet fully
recognized by the established medical experts, these alter-
natives are grounded in the history of their use and effec-
tiveness by many people in many cultures. Some of these
healing techniques are herbal supplements, flower essences
and essential oils, homeopathy, acupuncture, chakra align-
ments, various forms of bodywork, and psychospiritual inner processes such as meditation, contemplative prayer,
breathwork, and hypnosis.

Unless you are struggling with a physical illness, you
may not find this inner Healer to be of significance for you
at this time. For the selves already discussed carry the energies of Love, Wisdom, and Active Intelligence that bring forward our wounded pasts in ways that keep us healthy. And
in no manner is this deep archetypal work to ever take the
place of sound medical advice or treatment.

Your inner Healer works in conjunction with centers of
energy in your body, which are called **CHAKRAS**. In many
spiritual philosophies, chakras are thought of as rungs on
a ladder, the subtle energy "levels" we climb to build a
Self—or a metaphor for how we grow. Each chakra is related
to a physical location on the body, from the lowest at the
base of the spine to the uppermost on the top of the head.*

---

*A summary description and chart depicting the human chakra system
are given in Appendix 2, page 213.

The Inner Healer's Sacred Function

The purpose of this great subjective Helper is to magnetize, appropriate, and radiate the proper flow of energy, light, or power necessary to amplify one's healing process. The inner Healer works through the chakra closest to the afflicted area of the body.

When calling on your internal healing mechanism, it is important to remember that the Soul may have a goal for us concerning our life's plan that our intellects do not realize. It is not for us to question when one does not respond to a healing process—whether it be a conventional or an alternative method. The Soul may have completed what It came to do, and therefore is choosing a "way out." This is part of the mystery of Creation, a part we may never understand. It can be very calming, however, for people who are physically dying to recognize this fact. It gives meaning and sacred purpose to our suffering, and even to death.

EXERCISE: Summoning Your Inner Healer

This exercise is designed for two people working together, as if you are leading it for a friend who is struggling with illness of some sort. The process can, of course, be reversed, where someone else leads you through it. In either case, study the exercise thoroughly before attempting it.

Especially if the one who's hurting is responsive to music, you might accompany this process with some wordless transcendental or heartfelt orchestral music. The vibratory powers are healing on their own.

Throughout the process, both parties should maintain

an atmosphere of warmth, where you *feel* Love flowing between the two of you, as much as you can. This is especially important after you have said the co-creation prayer together.

Begin by sitting quietly with your friend, contemplating the troublesome situation that is causing the "dis-ease." Then start guiding the process by saying:

Settle into a comfortable position, close your eyes, and begin to relax by taking some slow, deep breaths.

Now start to speak aloud, free-associating about the ways your soul is longing to express itself in this concrete world, and how it has gone astray. . . . Let out any pent-up emotion—grief, rage, or existential angst about this situation. . . . Stay in these feelings— be with the process—for as long as you need to, as long as your energy expression continues.

It is crucial to release these loaded feelings, since physical ailment is often attached to unexpressed emotional pain or disillusionment, which may in itself actually be causing the illness.

Next have your friend say out loud with you: *We acknowledge one Creator. And we are aspects of this One. Therefore, we, as co-creators, have sacred powers that can assist in the healing process. We remove from the Law of Cause and Effect any conditions that are upholding this illness. We ask that the issue be resolved, through our willingness to cooperate with God's will, with Love.*

Allow a long pause here. If your friend is very weak, use your creative imagination to pass along some "life's blood." Loving Compassion and Nurturance are the greatest healers. These are not concepts; they are *powers*. So utilize these energies to their fullest extent.

Do not be afraid to offer your heart's Love, actually felt

as it flows through your own chest cavity into the other's. If you are a *magnetic* healer, you will transfer your energy to them (as they may be too weak to access their own inner Healer). If you are a *radiatory* healer, you can amplify more of their own power source, so they can do this work for themselves.

Stay non-attached, yet completely present, and feeling, with enhanced heartfelt energies for the sake of your friend. You are ''turning up the heat.'' But remember to retain your own sense of Self always, and do not get lost in the other.

After a period of quiet, continue the process by saying: *Now call for your Healing Angel to appear in your subjective reality. . . . See, hear, or feel the energy as it surrounds you. And ask for guidance from this inner Healer.*

Hold the silence for quite a while. Then proceed: *In the presence of this healing energy, breathe in light, and breathe out the suffering or pain, relaxing more and more as the healing process takes hold. Keep relaxing . . . more and more deeply . . . knowing that healing happens in the silence of our minds and hearts.*

When the two of you are back once more in this ordinary reality, take some time to discuss what just occurred. Before ending, be sure to acknowledge and thank the inner Healer. For the feeling of gratitude is also a healing power. And— especially if you are a magnetic healer—be sure that you as the guide have disidentified from the other's process.

Embracing All Our Selves

Now you have met the many ''selves'' who can oper- ate separately or together within our human psyches to make us whole. These are archetypes (human blueprints), which are there for our use at all times, even though they're often below the surface of our conscious awareness. As are many others—such as Warrior, Magician, Artist, Divine Mother, and on and on. Let your own creativity flourish as you think about this rich inner life of yours. And draw on any archetype you feel is specifically appropriate for any given situation. For now, though, the basic selves mentioned here can carry you forward toward a combined goal of healing yourselves and helping others.

You can learn to call on whichever archetype you need for activating a certain function, or for strengthening whatever aspect of yourself needs a little boost. Practice using your intuition to call them out, and make a commitment to get to know them intimately. You'll be surprised at all the gifts awaiting you—far more than these mere words could ever express!

Making conscious the archetypal reality "just beyond this earth life" is one of the greatest aspects of our journey Home. It actually reconnects us with the gods and goddesses of old, who, like us, are evolving. They are our link to wholeness, as they contain qualities and powers we've forgotten *we* have—that can now be accessed through our creative imaginations. And we, as humans, contain experiences through our awakened physical senses that these greater Beings love to access as well. Therefore, the doorway between this ordinary reality and the archetypal dimension is currently open, as our human and beyond-human selves come together to move us forward along our path of unfolding.

The Importance of Shadow Work

First Things First

Many conscientious people today are deeply concerned about the environment and other troubles on our planet. But we needn't feel hopeless about the immensity of the unhealthy conditions, thinking that one person can't make a difference. On the contrary, quite the opposite is true. The work of theoretical biologist Rupert Sheldrake teaches that when a certain behavior is repeated often enough, it becomes easier and easier for the rest of the species to follow suit. What a powerful motivation for each of us to do just "our part"!

The first step in global healing, then, is to work toward healing our *individual* wounded and unconscious shadows. We start by looking behind us to see who is following along, too immature to keep up, because it is this still uncivilized part in us who causes so much pain and suffering in the world.

In order to acknowledge this dark side of human nature, we must ask our shadows to come forward and show themselves. The reclaiming of our lost and disowned self starts with this simple step of admitting that we *have* a "dark side."

So the beginning of inner work is to own all our "stuff" instead of allowing it to harm others through projection. **PROJECTION** is a tactic we use when not claiming those repressed shadow parts. Through projection, we see in others —*and act out in ways that humiliate us*—the very traits we dislike most. When perceiving these things in others, we become reactive to them, not realizing that we are despising the very same traits in ourselves.

An obsessive outer focus on unresolved issues leaves us little time to recognize and develop our true gifts and spiritual inheritance. Many people unconsciously remain stuck in the past with their addictions, attachments, and limited story lines, while their shadows keep growing bigger.

Therefore, all work of a psychospiritual nature begins with "shadow work," a regression back into the past to accept, heal, and forgive any aspects of our experience where we've taken on wounding and limitation. To heal means "to make whole" (holy), and wholeness has no missing parts. This work often includes a re-examination of old taken-for-granted beliefs that have come from our family traditions, religious training, or other orthodoxies.

To be true "spiritual warriors" at this turning of the evolutionary wheel, we must all come out of denial concerning any of our "lopsided parts." We're required to make conscious our own descent into "the underworlds" of egoistic separatism, selfishness, and ignorance. Our soul, who through innocence has gotten trapped in matter, needs retrieval. Until we can fully understand and heal what we personally have been through, we have little chance of helping others or healing the planet.

Clearing the human psyche of all its clutter and unconscious ways will eventually lead to a better world, for it's the human psyche who images and perceives the world. Once cleared, we will be able to enter the higher spiritual realities without distorting these higher dimensions with our own egoistic desires.

In this way, we become "free karmic agents," and can function on any plane of reality by our commitment to Spirit. But this work is hard to do without building a good bridge between the lower and higher worlds. Just as the heart bridges dualism and unification, so does *individual* shadow work lead to *global* salvation.

Shadow Tracking

Because the human shadow plays such an important role in the current world condition and its healing, it deserves a thorough review. The information given next expands on the earlier description of problems inherent in the human conditon. Specifically, it explains how unhealthy parenting is a breeding ground for "shadow-making."

As already discussed, the human learning process doesn't begin when we land on the delivery table; rather, our first school room is the mother's womb. As unborn babies, we learn by experience, through our whole being, during the nine months before birth. While in the womb, we absorb both the physical and the emotional issues of our mothers. And, unfortunately, this kind of holistic learning is the hardest to correct later, because it has been imprinted throughout our being, in our very cells.

Once we are born, the problems multiply. When parents

need children for an emotional sense of worthiness or ego strength, they make unrealistic demands. Their tiny offspring are expected to be perfect and always shine, exemplifying to others the values and supposed worth of the family.

Some children live amid so much emotional drama, they learn from their grown-up family members that fighting and abusing one another can lead to making up romantically, with passionate love-making. In such cases, unchecked shadows take hold of the family dynamics, making the younger members dysfunctional carriers of these patterns into their own relationships later on.

Children in alcoholic families learn from the addicts how to escape through substances, and from the co-dependent relatives how to control and manipulate. Others grow up with parents in troubled marriages, where one parent turns to the child for nurturing and support, creating a syndrome called "emotional incest." And some parents sexually abuse their children, leaving them with deep emotional scars and seriously distorted messages about sexuality and love.

These are the kinds of terribly damaging scenarios many grow up with, everything from "you're here for my pleasure" to "drink or drug 'til you feel numb." Children easily take these ideas for granted, assuming them to be true because "they" said so. This is how robotic habits set in, then follow us, unexamined, through life.

Brought up on such values, and adults' expectations of being unnaturally quiet, a child's normal emotions spawn shadows. Reacting to criticism for simply being natural, children learn to feel undeserved shame. Not knowing enough to question the authority of those whose approval they

crave, they believe the negativity, and turn against themselves. Gradually over the years, the particular image taken
on to please others becomes well developed, a solid false
persona. And we learn to bury, and disown, those parts of
us that do not fit the ideal persona—those masks we wear
for our families' and society's approval. This is the shadow.

It's up to each of us to make conscious the damaging
false beliefs, and change them when they no longer fit.
Otherwise, every time one of them triggers an automatic
response, the shadow gains strength. Though it is still
deeply repressed underneath the weight of the untruth, it
takes on a life of its own, the not-self. No healthy Self can
be built on such an illusory foundation.

Our Three Basic Levels of Ego Consciousness

Another way of looking at the problematic shadow is to
review human ego development as it evolves through a ser-
ies of levels. The physical, emotional, and mental levels are
usually thought of as the beginning of this normal process,
the three together considered to be our basic personality.
Although it may sound linear, the actual unfolding is really
more like a spiraling in and out and around all the stages in
no set sequence. Yet our most basic, core unmet needs always drop us down to the lowest level.

Studying the first three levels of human growth clearly
shows how dysfunctional addictive patterns come about as
a defense against the damaging treatment many of us were
subjected to early in life. Each level contains certain quali-

ties of living and specific trials we must undergo in order to develop.

The first level is **physical** consciousness. While establishing a basic sense of security in the world, some of us have become over-controlling of ourselves and others in order to feel safe. Though developed long ago out of need—the most basic need for physical well-being—in current times these shadows are likely to be activated whenever our security is threatened.

During the second stage, while our **emotional-relational** lives were developing, we may have built up shadows that withhold feelings, or distract us through melodrama when we are threatened by intimacy or unmet emotional or relational needs.

Any exaggerated feeling or over-reaction is an indicator that some unconscious unmet emotional need has been activated by an outer stimulus. These shadows often overtake our love lives, or our relationships to authority figures. Whatever it is that the wound in the past miscreated, this is the sounding note that moves the shadow today.

And as if the first two stages aren't demanding enough on their own, the ego's architecture is *hierarchical* in nature, meaning that the higher includes the lower, but the lower does not include the higher. Therefore, when a distortion occurs at Level 1, it is carried forward to Level 2 where it takes on more discoloration and emotional force; and all this dysfunciton is brought into Level 3, the **mental** life, where we carry our ideas about ourselves—such as our self-esteem or self-image.

Here the ego may have bloomed in all its radiance as

some sort of warped personality, so that now it can function autonomously. This leaves us with intellects ruled by whatever is the resultant mixture of unhealthy or unrealistic ideas, attitudes, and values; or with egos that are too protective to allow us to really live.

These kinds of impaired development produce all our addictions and dysfunctional ways of living. When recognized, faced, and turned around, however, these imbalanced urges are transmuted into our highest and most wondrous spiritual qualities, for they've been earned from our experience. For travelers on "the journey to wholeness," they are the substance of things valued, our avenues to completion and unconditional love.

EXERCISE: **Correcting "Self-Talk"**

Listening to your "self-talk" allows you to hear examples of your own mental imbalances so you can correct them. For instance, you may hear yourself continually defending any apparent attack on your ideas or beliefs; you may be caring too much about whether you are always right or without fault. Or you may discover you are in the habit of putting yourself down or discounting your successes.

Start off by spending one full day focusing on how you talk to people about yourself. Pay particular attention to your responses to their comments *pertaining to you. After doing this once, you might want to repeat it at regular intervals, perhaps once a week for a while. Decrease or increase the frequency of practice as you become more familiar with your patterns, or the triggers that cause your imbalances.*

Your Observer Self can be a great help with this exercise in consciousness, and much self-awareness can come from it. This practice aids not only you, but anyone you come in contact with as well, especially those you guide.

Tending to the Shadow

We all have some degree of shadowy dysfunction woven into the fabric of our identities, which give us pockets of lopsidedness and fragility. In the journey toward wholeness, both the ego and the shadow are honored as valuable parts of us, and are put to use at their highest capacity.

Remember, when we were younger, our egos became our closest friends by developing the defenses necessary to help us survive the strain of dysfunctional families and other factors. Then as we were continually wounded, our egos carefully wove themselves around these wounds, creating stronger and stronger defensive blocks, just as a physical wound creates a scab for protection while it heals. Conscious psychological healing later on requires a purification of these places in our wounded psyches that are contaminating us. And this should be done without shame or being shamed by anyone else. For we all have scars from our childhoods. None of us had fully enlightened parents!

Our healing is *never about* attacking the shadow or trying to kill it off. We don't wish to destroy our passionate nature, or tame it into non-expression. How very dull this would make us! Instead, we want to learn to *contain* these amazing creative energies and use them for a higher good.

But until shadow material is acknowledged and mostly integrated, we can never really access our spiritual, but uncreated, wholeness.

Retrieving Our Lost Parts

When we first turn within and begin to question who we really are, the healthy ego moves in and takes us back through our past to "clean house." We're required to uncover any "uncooked seeds" that are still being carried around, still holding back some of our vital energies, locked up in dysfunctional patterns. We must clear out each "story of the house," so we can move on.

As we recognize and study these old issues through memory and reflection, we start "separating the wheat from the chaff" among all the experiences. This return to the past offers the opportunity to take a fresh look through the eyes of the more evolved person we've now become. We can better see what the past and its key players in our lives have really meant, in terms of our soul's development. This type of inner work is sometimes called "soul retrieval."

At times during this reevaluation, we might become emotional for no apparent reason. Even so, we should always try to fully experience whatever sensations or feelings arise, especially any over-reactions—for the over-reactions point to our most wounded and "stuck" places. And since the true healer and true authority lives within us, opening up to what's inside is how we heal. We must always honor our thoughts and intuitive wisdom as the insights come along.

To come fully awake, we take responsibility for remaining conscious, not allowing ourselves to fall into any sort of denial of what is trying to be revealed. If something becomes unsettling, it means that a healing process has been activated. So pain must be welcomed, for if it's "up," it's on its way out. An old saying wisely tells us: "If you can't feel it, you can't heal it."

Healers of the future know how to gently guide their clients back through the troubled times experientially. This way they can relive the traumatic events while looking through the lens of understanding and forgiveness, then move on beyond guilt or shame about *anything* human. After all, since it's *human* we are learning to be, obviously we will fall short now and then.

EXERCISE: **Balancing a Lopsidedness**

Whenever you find yourself falling into one of your old unhealthy patterns, take some time, sit down quietly, go within, and connect with your Observer. As a neutral witness, it can point out what's going on. Then you can restore balance by following these steps:

Identify the person inside who is reacting badly to the situation, and get an image.

Once this is visualized, begin to communicate with the image, letting it say what it needs. Ask it to bring forth its opposite partner, its positive counterpart. Then take time to observe through the inner eye who appears on the scene as this opposite one.

For example, if a pouty child with hurt feelings was the first image, perhaps the positive partner will be the Divine Child. It is important to stay spontaneous and trust the imagination as these symbols come.

Once the positive side is clear (the one you were denying), name its qualities. Naming them is the beginning of crystalizing this counterpart into reality.

Now allow the two sides of you to merge (the pouty child and the Divine Child), and see who emerges as the third. Then take this new and higher image into your ordinary life, and live as this one.

Getting an image of the third and higher being might be easier if you first picture a triangle. Now see the two opposite counterparts sitting across from one another at the triangle's two bottom corners. Then, when these two have merged, the third image appears at the top of the triangle.

With inner work such as this, a transformation takes place *spontaneously* within the psyche. In the example above, the little hurt child and its partner are energetically transformed into One Self: The positive qualities of the Divine child (like a fresh and open innocence) are combined with the passion that was repressed in the shadow side.

Now with neither side of the polarity being denied, you're balanced and living from a higher level of consciousness as that "third and greater one," another step closer to your true Self. This type of inner work brings relief, and often a great amount of new self-understanding as well.*

---

*Another exercise for working with the Observer Self is given in the last chapter, page 82.

Living from Center

The previous exercise is a method we can use to find the balance in all pairs of opposites like work/play, selfish/un-selfish, childlike/mature, etc. It shows us how to think in terms of "both/and," and how to grow from this kind of thinking. We learn to pull into shape something new and higher that is on the periphery of emergence, holding steady while in the midst of the clearing process. This is the way to balance our lopsidedness.

Holding steady is the tricky part, as it requires conscious attention to the difficult task at hand. Whenever trying to balance two opposing polarities, we should be aware of the tension between the two opposite poles. This means that the original perspective exerts a strong emotional pull at the same time as we're bringing to light the value of its oppo-site. We need to respect our natural feelings of resistance, and to recognize just how stressful this balancing act can be. But it's worth the effort, for this is how we become centered, how we learn to live within the **TENSION OF THE OPPOSITES**.

Learning to "live from center" creates the freedom of a contrasting design. We can move in whatever way the energies of the moment sway us, flowing this way and that in open-mindedness, and not becoming rigid at any point. For now that we are no longer trying to prove anything by doggedly staying at one pole or the other, we no longer have anything to get rigid about!

Like "riding a rainbow," we allow whatever "color" pours through to have its natural expression. We are just be-ing ourselves, with total acceptance of what is, never acting like experts on either side of the equation, and always keeping an eye of compassion wide open to expose the overview. Once we become this self-accepting, we can learn to love and accept others as well. But not before! The degree of our own healing determines the degree of our loving nature in all our relationships.

Even when we're consciously following a path of inner healing, the human experience gives us two approaches: We can enter into the dance of the opposites, willing to take on whatever life brings, and experience it all the way through, sometimes even in an exaggerated (and humiliating) state. Or we can learn to live from center, deliberately rising above those aspects of life we choose *not* to enter into. Both ways can lead to growth. The healthier choice, however, is from the center, where we don't have to hook into everything that's going on around us. This means keeping the Observer Self intact and operative in our daily lives.

From center, we can simultaneously be both the onlooker and the experiencer, and thereby become more selective about when to ''play ourselves into life'' and when to remain uninvolved. We can conserve our precious energy for the sacred work of transformation, and not waste it on melodrama. For, whatever we focus on and give our passion to becomes our reality. As conscious beings, we have free choice.

Switching Priorities

Tuning into the Inner Life

Making the shift from outer distractions to inner essence is the order of the day. In our emerging reality, we will no longer be so predisposed to outward seeking. We'll no longer gain our identity so much by *doing*, but more from simply *being* who we are. Modeling how to just be ourselves helps others discover this freedom as well. You might say that this service of "doing your being," is not only the way we ourselves grow, but also how we help others. This shift from *outer form* to *inner essence* honors the wisdom within us all. It is the self-mastery stance.

The world inside is always trying to reveal its greater Mind to us. We need only to learn how it communicates, so we can recognize our subjective images and feelings as real, and trust them. As we practice "going within," we gradually realize how connected we already are to our own inherent wisdom. The powers of Higher Mind begin to activate through new forms of cognition that take us "beyond intellect."

This inner life of Higher Mind is composed of the *creative imagination, inspiration,* and *intuition*. In addition, we can learn to utilize another soul power, that of the Higher Will, which we might not realize we have. It is called *invocation*.

Using these powers rounds out our lives in ways that truly gratify the soul.

Following next are definitions of these higher aspects of our human/divine nature. They are given here to provide a better understanding of how we can use the mind and our human will to put into effect these more holistic qualities for enhancing our growth. All transformation begins with the inner life!

The Powers of Higher Mind

CREATIVE IMAGINATION is our mind's ability to image (or put into form) a desired thought or ideal. It is our inner picture-making ability. When our imaginative cognition awakens, we "see" more in inner images that come into our minds spontaneously. This is a warm flowing cognition, not "dry" the way intellectualism sometimes feels.

We can never have what we cannot imagine! And when people can no longer envision a desired future, all hope dies, and the people perish. Creative imagination is therefore our most cherished soul power. By comparison, strict intellectualism falls flat and is *not* transformative. No energy is exchanged.

To manifest something we've imagined, we bring what we want to create into our feelings, and *will ourselves* to feel the intention all through our bodies, minds, and hearts. For anything new to be created, mental energy, a strong desire, and a willingness to pursue must all be present simultaneously.

When both your mind and heart are behind your intention, you can overcome the "stuck" feeling of a troublesome situation by picturing its favorable resolution. Converting frustration into empowerment happens by simply using your mind, as "thinking it" arouses the forces that bring it on. Here's a short keynote to summarize this point: *Energy follows thought.*

[AUTHOR ANECDOTE FROM MARY] *Several years ago, I was in the throes of buying a house I'd found after considerable searching. Knowing how unpredictable real estate transactions can be, and not taking anything for granted, I put creative imagination to work. Every night I'd drop off to sleep visualilzing how my furniture would fit in, and how I'd decorate that particular house. And it did soon become mine.*

INSPIRATION is a divine influence on a human being, a stimulus to creative thought or action. The origin of its base word, *inspire*, is "to breathe life into," or "have an animating effect on," something previously inert. An inspired thought is fueled by the fires of Spirit, a message and "spark" that drop in from a Higher Order, impressing our brains in ways that stimulate us beyond ordinary thinking.

So inspiration is like intuition in the sense that it triggers action based on something other than an intellectual decision. An inspiration is a *felt* shift we experience as a "quickening" in our hearts. As we put more faith in the inner life, this too can be trusted as a valid source of direction. It reminds us that we are connected to—indeed, are mediators for—a bigger story, through both our minds and our hearts.

INTUITION is more subtle than inspiration, the sense of a quiet *direct knowing* of something that comes on suddenly without the conscious use of reasoning. It always shows us something about our place in our Creator's greater Plan for us. Intuition is an immediate understanding that can't always be explained logically. This can be a hunch about an impending decision, a sense or feeling that seems to tell which action is preferable.

The intuition comes from an accumulation of wisdom gained from all our life's experiences. Learning to trust the inner messages of our intuitive knowing is a key element of keeping us on track according to our own life's purpose and plan. As healing professionals advance toward the new ways, intuitive wisdom—their own *and* that of their clients —will be honored more and more.

The Power of Higher Will

Our final soul power relates to co-creation, which you've already read about in Part 1. A more complete definition of **CO-CREATION** is *a willing participation in the making of our world conditions*. As sons and daughters of a Creator God, by our very nature, we too are creative. So we are always either consciously co-creating or unconsciously *mis*-creating.

Co-creation takes place when our spiritual will is aligned with the good of the whole to help create and fulfill our individual roles on earth. Once aware that we are both human and divine, we can take more responsibility for our lives.

The power of Higher Will, **INVOCATION**, is co-creative or *active* prayer. Rather than praying to an external God, we call on our own ''god nature,'' the God within, for the guidance we need to effect changes. This stance carries a willingness to do "our part," to make a contribution toward the outcome by consciously invoking the wisdom of a Higher Power. This is like saying, "I'm willing, *and* I need guidance. Send me my instructions, and I'll follow through."

But we must remember that invoking something sets it into motion. Always be careful about what you ask for, as it will surely come to be! When we invoke something, we are calling it to us. Then we start attracting the tests that train us for the new. Invoking patience, for example, can bring on many unwelcome experiences that *try our patience* while we practice becoming one who embodies the archetypal quality of Patience.

Exercise: **I Am Willing . . . !**

Reflect on something new you would like to have in your life. Perhaps it is more of a certain quality, such as freedom or success. Or perhaps you desire a new experience.

Once you've selected what you wish to invoke, go to a quiet place—outside in nature if possible. Now face eastward, to symbolize new life dawning in "the East" where the sun always rises.

Hold up both arms over your head, stretching toward the heavens and, with all your might, say to God, "I am willing to have_____in my life, and to take full responsibility for it!"

Next—with resolution—bring your arms back down to your sides, as though you have actually taken this new thing or quality down out of the heavens and placed it into your body. An attitude of both complete conviction and intensity of yearning is crucial.

Once you've done this, release the yearning, and put the whole subject out of your mind. You have done ''your part,'' and have given it to God in total faith in this process.

Letting Go of Disempowering Patterns

If we do not recognize our own creative potential, we are giving away our power. We're left living out our precious lives in a dependent, disempowered state, believing others are more important or more talented than we are, our powers of Higher Mind remaining latent and unrecognized aspects of our nature. This lack of self-development and creative expression blocks our connection with the inner life. We're so busy doing what others tell us to do, we have no free attention left over for going within and hearing the still, small voice of our soul who holds the key to our fulfillment.

Acting in codependent ways that depend on outer authority is what leads us to forget about the ''God within,'' seeking an external God. We see Him as an ''old man in the sky''—an empty form, a pure illusion—who rewards us when we're good and punishes us when we're bad, according to how *our egos* have been programmed to perceive morality.

In other words, the ego, through its child-like ignorance, has created a troublesome man-made God, and allowed sleepy, robotic mass consciousness to tell us what to value and call real. Through exclusive schools of religion, which were designed to control an immature humanity, we've invented this patriarchal, judgmental God and made Him the ultimate Authority for our lives. You might humorously call this "cosmic codependence."

As the old order based on patriarchal outer authority collapses, we must be prepared for a "destiny transfer," which is experienced as a total shake-up of the lives we've known, and the identities we are used to being.

We are moving into a whole new dimension of the Self, where the entire concept or story line that has been holding our reality in place is coming to a screeching halt. We are being required now to make the shift from outer to inner focus, to rediscover the most ancient of truths: All we ever need to know or be is already built within us, as the children of a living Creator God.

It isn't easy to release old patterns and let go of emotional attachments stuck to us like our very skin, however. Here's a sacred exercise that can help.

EXERCISE: **Healing a Lingering Attachment**

Set up a small bowl with a burning candle in the center, and half full of water. If possible, sprinkle some flower petals on the water's surface. You'll also need a small piece of paper, something to write with, a pair of tweezers, and a matchbook or lighter. Now you are ready to begin.

Think of something or someone you feel is holding you back, something you want to give up. It might be fear, depression, self-doubt, . . . or an old relationship you can't seem to release. NOTE: If it's an unhealthy relationship with a person, find words to describe your attachment—for this is what you'll be surrendering, not the actual person.

Once you have decided the specific attachment you are ready to give up, write it down on the paper. Concentrate intensely on what this attachment has meant for you. . . . Remember as much detail as you can, both the positives and the negatives you associate with it.

When you feel complete with this reflection, wad up the paper into a tight ball. Then, standing in front of the bowl in deep contemplation, light the paper and quickly pick up a corner of it with the tweezers. As you watch the paper turn to embers, envision this attachment leaving you.

Before the paper disintegrates completely, drop it into the bowl, its burial ground, and notice the shape it becomes in the water. Feel compassion for this sacrificed thing as it leaves you. And feel a new-found freedom in your heart. You might want to take the charred remnants to a quiet place outside, and actually bury it in the ground. End the process in gratitude for the lesson learned, and your ability to release.

"Hanging in the Dangle"

At those times when everything in our lives seems to be falling away, we are in the sacred process of "disidentification," witnessing the death of an outlived way of being. Our intellectual concepts that have always held us together no longer work. But we haven't begun to completely trust our inner images and intuitive hunches as valid. This feels like "hanging in the dangle" between a world that is rapidly dying and one that's not quite taken form yet.

For an uncomfortable period of time, we feel there's no foundation underneath our feet; we are suspended in space and time. And no matter how hard we try to go back and do things in the old way, they just don't work anymore.

Sound familiar? Perhaps you're feeling this right now. Thousands everywhere are currently undergoing this "death/rebirth" experience, which the ancients called "the dark night of the soul."

In order for us to have room for anything new to happen in our lives, however, we must let go of the old. So at certain stages in our growth cycles, we are required by a "higher law" to release *in form and content* all that we've been attached to or gained our identities from, during the cycle that is ending.

But as the content or form dissolves, the *essence* is squeezed out of the experiences we've undergone and this essence is carried forward; all the temporal parts are forgotten or forgiven, in love and with an understanding of each one's higher purpose. For example, we may have to undergo some form of great loss. Although we grieve, the compassion we've gained from our suffering carries forward; we're now more willing to serve others. This is how we sift out the "gold" from each experience, allowing the "dross" of all the non-essential content to fall away. So nothing of true value is ever really lost—only our illusions and old, dead forms. We carry forward that which is eternal.

As we consciously review our lives from "the Bigger Picture" of *real* Reality, we absorb the essentials gained from every personal involvement. We're able to see meaningful lessons in all of it. And whatever is exposed during this review that is not to be carried forward into the next cycle is called out so it can be named and released. To name something is to disidentify with it: It's held out in front and

looked squarely in the eye, seen through our Observer consciousness as *not* who we are. And with no judgment, we
simply turn and walk away.

Perhaps we see that we've been involved in situations
concerning possessiveness, or greed, or irresponsibility. Or
maybe this has been a financially successful time containing
many temptations to dig more deeply into the materialistic
side of life.

No matter what experiences we unearth, we must remember that they are not *who we are*; the experiences are just
the challenges and trials we had to butt up against to test our
mettle. It is our unifying Higher Self who is doing this work.

This higher Transpersonal Self is larger than its conditions always, the bedrock on which all our "personhood"
is based. It knows how to see patterns in their entirety, and
has no need to get all caught up in the content of each passing detail. To the Self, who lives on a higher plane, all those
little separate vignettes we've passed through gather into
clusters of meaningful events; and each has as its essential
quality a lesson or "gift" that helps refine us into a closer
approximation of our own Ideal.

Especially if you are responsible for guiding others,
you'll do well to keep in mind that perhaps the most crucial
element of anyone's healing is to recognize our human trials
as lessons in refinement and growth, which we all require.
This helps clients release the shame that binds them to their
pasts. When people are trapped in feelings of shame, they
are unable to look inward and face the unfinished past. They
defend, deflect, or go into denial anytime one of those old
buttons gets punched. Using self-disclosure—with discre-

tion—helps your clients see that you too have made mistakes and have unfinished issues of your own, that you are human.*

Learning to be more open and honest with those we guide is a trend in psychotherapy today. We are moving away from those old "over/under" relationships where therapists are supposed to be experts on clients' growth. Now they are more like elder brothers and sisters—guides who share their own journeys, not authorities who "know" what's best for another.

A Search for Meaning and Purpose

We're being called to a whole new way of knowing that comes more from the intuition than from logic, more from the wisdom of our experience than from knowledge found in theories and books. As our priorities continue to shift, we're in for an all-encompassing "about-face" in perspective, from a taken-for-granted attitude about what is right and wrong to one of inner questioning. This is a deep, soul-searching experiential process, a search for meaning and purpose.

We still honor our pasts—the lessons learned and the people who have played important roles in our lives—but now we are to integrate it all and stop looking back. We begin to listen and align with higher ideals. We look ahead,

---

*The concept of self-disclosure is fully discussed in Part 3, beginning on page 134.

and take a more *proactive* view of who we are, with no more need to be *reactive* to the past. When we widen our focus, we see that we are much bigger than we'd thought.

To connect with our greater Self and the patterns just beyond us, we must go within to "hear our instructions" and be willing to become more future-directed—knowing always that we won't find the answers outside us anywhere. All new creative visions, inspirations, and insights come from within. And it's a great adventure to turn inward, for all kinds of treasures are awaiting us there! Having recognized God inside us, our inner lives are enhanced immeasurably. Now we see that all potential and sacred purpose resides in our own minds and hearts.

Ready to help us gain our new perspective is the Observer Self, who becomes connected to our daily routines. With the eyes of a hawk, Observer notes everything we do, poking us to be sure that we "see" and "hear" what really matters through the senses of our essential nature, the Heart.

Remember that observing something, as the quantum physicists say, automatically changes it. We cannot become aware of something and make it conscious without experiencing an inner change; and changes often taken place in our outer lives as well. "While doing the Work of *that* world, we 'eat the bread' of *this* world." And we learn.

As we travel this journey, our compassion for all we meet along the way leads us into **RIGHT RELATIONSHIP**. This is about every person finding his or her own true place and spiritual purpose within the collective (within each specific relationship and within the universe as a whole). Like individual pieces of a puzzle, each of us takes responsibility for one part. Each person fills in one authentic and unique place in the big picture, our Creator's Plan, not leaving any gaps or leaning too heavily into another's rightful space.

Everyone contributes to the finished design, and all together illustrate that they are members of a sacred family of souls, all of equal status, uniting to create a grand design. All are free to move into the higher life they are co-creating, separately and together. Passions and yearnings are no longer directed toward ego games.

The Law of Sacrifice is the ruler of right relationship. It governs how "the part" (ego) finds its true and perfect relationship within "the whole" (God, or Ultimate Reality). But "sacrifice" isn't as negative as we've come to believe. The word itself comes from the root word *sacr-*, which means "to make holy." The gradual process of surrender to a Higher Power is endless, though, for we never stop moving to higher and higher destinies, always sacrificing the lesser for the greater. Every time we fixate on something or someone in *this* world on the horizontal plane, we are required to let go and return to *that* higher world to gain a perspective. Otherwise we suffer.

People "on the path" are warned about suffering, because it is *real. And it hurts.* But it never stops the true seeker from aspiring toward a higher way. The complementarity of being *in* the world and not *of* it is how we learn to undergo this continual process with grace.

Our progress as we move from fragmented egos to soul-centered personalities is always a very personal matter, since the ratio between ego energy and soul energy varies from person to person and event to event. It all depends on the lessons accepted and learned, and how far we have already come along the way of self-development, responsibility, and love.

Shifting from competitiveness to creativity, we are always in the process of stripping away old parts of ourselves that are no longer useful. Gradually we become more and more centered, as we learn to live fully in the present moment. The past can no longer be a priority once this process of inner transformation ensues. From now on, the future calls us to unfold into our true and full expression as spiritual beings in human form—in each moment, in the eternal *now*. We move on!

As this new millennium dawns, we have a unique opportunity. An ''about face'' in human consciousness is ushering in a new identification for us and for our world. Now is the time to make our amends, pay our debts, and clear out old dead patterns. Then we can head for new shores with the creative aliveness that naturally comes with being just who we are—transparent, expectant, and wholly accepting of our next right step.

What an exciting challenge! When we make a commitment, looking beyond those old ''wrinkles in time'' of our outworn past, and opening to the possibilities that await our discovery, we can't help seeing a future that invites us forward. We need only expand our vision to include the *inner* life—our soul's entire psychospiritual reality. A return to the original Self is—always and already—our purpose and true destiny.

Part 3

Sharing Ourselves as Role Models
• New Implications in the Work •

Research has proven that effective "people-helpers" have a number of naturally therapeutic traits in common. These qualities stem from the universal law of love, *the transformational law*, which is the driving force behind our essence. This means that love is truth. When people communicate in truth, a noticeable exchange of energy takes place. And when they don't, no energy is exchanged—no healing happens.

Awakened healers of the future cultivate these therapeutic qualities and the ability to use certain methods that assist others in releasing their uncomfortable, often devastating, conditions. And besides assisting their clients, the new-consciousness helpers demonstrate their authenticity in all facets of their lives.

By continually being effective within their specific spheres of influence, they are remodeling the outmoded mainstream methods that no longer work. In this way, the healing spreads not only through individual and group counseling but all through the community, and beyond.

Characteristics of
Effective Healers

When Less Is More

As evolution reaches beyond the limited old views of the past, and we make the shift away from outer *form* to inner *essence*, we learn about the qualities that make a difference, such as authenticity, openmindedness, and creativity. External "shoulds" and the need to achieve goals are dropped, being replaced by the inner work that brings us depth, faith, perseverance, harmlessness, strength of character, and spiritual stature—in other words, empowerment of the true Self. It's all about just settling into ourselves and realizing that we're loveable; not only are we loveable, we're also naturally wise. And our goals are achieved more easily when we are self-empowered.

An *untrained* person who listens from the heart (as opposed to the intellect) often has a much more healing effect than those who have trained themselves to "be helpful." Some of the most educated people have lost their inherent therapeutic abilities. It's as though these natural human responses were *trained right out of them*. And research in human psychology has actually borne this out.*

*For information on these studies, refer to *Becoming Naturally Therapeutic* ("References") by Jacquelyn Small.

Distancing themselves from the pain of others and trying to act like experts are two ways psychotherapists frequently get into trouble—not only with their clients, but with themselves as well. These professional hazards are often simply a result of the therapist's ignorance about how real therapeutic healing happens.

Most professional counselors have been taught to remain aloof, sitting efficiently behind their desks, staying neatly and appropriately clad in "counselor clothing." This attitude literally allows distance to separate them from those in need. But even worse, some professionals in this field fall into the category of "the codependent helper." They throw their personal ego weaknesses and unfinished psychological business at the client, or over-identify with the client's issues as a way to avoid looking at their own.

But it isn't just the professional psychotherapist who can come across as a lecturer, preacher, savior, or judge—all toxic ways of relating! Everyone is in danger of hiding behind roles that block the essence of true helping. And we all intuitively know when we are being subjected to someone's "laying a trip" on us too. It's the heart that knows. For the heart is a built-in "truth detector," even though we don't always listen, often allowing others to take advantage of us.

Something within us is beginning to rise up in dissatisfaction with those who insist on calling us sick or crazy, and who don't seem to remember how to "come from the heart." Clients of professional therapists are changing, reclaiming their right to be human and to expect human responses. They are tiring of being viewed through the lens of pathology. And so are we all! We want and deserve the same level of respect, regardless of our errors and pain.

Therapeutic relating occurs when both parties have dissolved the distinction between the one needing help and the one offering it. Instead, while respecting certain boundaries as appropriate to the professional relationship, they consider themselves two beings "bouncing off" each other in truth. The light of love enters when truth happens. Love is truth, and truth is *power*—the power to be real, or realized. Truth is the *power to be.*

When a therapist willingly accepts this all-too-human role of truthful openness rather than a superior role of teaching, a genuine healing process ensues. The most helpful counselors are those who come from their hearts, making use of the naturally therapeutic qualities and methods discussed next.

These ways of dealing with people in healing situations are divided among three categories: *supporting, challenging,* and *total-way-of-being* qualities.

• • •

A Note about the Dialogs: This section uses both client/counselor and non-professional examples from everyday life—interactions between family members and friends. As you read along, let this serve as a reminder that therapeutic relating applies in all our relations—for we all have hearts, and certainly we all have troubles.

Qualities That Support

Showing support for a client comes naturally when we're living in the heart. With feeling, we establish a solid rapport by being down-to-earth, honest, and open to whatever the situation requires. The five "supporting" qualities found in high-functioning counselors are *empathy, genuineness, respect, self-disclosure,* and *warmth*.

EMPATHY

This is the quality of perceiving another's experience and then communicating back that perception. A listener hears, and without feeling the other's feelings, begins to get a mental picture of the essence of what is being described. These perceptions are then verbalized, using "I" language to own the perceptions rather than "putting words into the other's mouth."

THE SCENARIO

JOAN: With head down, arms crossed, squeezing her chest in a constricted fashion, "I just can't . . . can't take it. They all want me to. . . . Oh, I don't see how I can . . ."

FRIEND: "I hear your pain, Joan. You seem so sad. And look how you're clenching your fists as you talk about it. It's as though your family's strangling you. Some sort of struggle for breath is what I'm sensing."

THE PROCESS

The friend tries not to analyze or interpret, but to simply listen for the total message, observing ''body language'' and other meaning below the surface of what's being said.

As they talk, the friend draws closer to Joan. In this way, a counselor would verbally and nonverbally allow clients to feel respected and heard.

The friend makes ''I'' statements, making it clear that he's talking about his own impressions, so that Joan can see how she's coming across. This non-judgmental feedback keeps her from becoming defensive. This is important because Joan remains free to accept or reject the perceptions being portrayed.

The healing element of this empathy-in-action is *not* the accuracy of the listener's perceptions. It is the intense and caring interaction between the two. The most positive communication takes place on a subterranean, therapeutic level—within the relationship itself.

THE OPPOSITE

Here are some examples of people who react *without* empathy:

1) A listener who presents his or her perceptions *as facts*. This adds confusion and takes others further away from their own truths.

2) One who analyzes a sharer's situation or dynamics as if an expert on the other's inner experience. This goes against the new way of thinking that the healer is within, that an outsider *doesn't* know best.

3) Counselors who cannot give full attention to their clients. This happens most often when therapists are too preoccupied with personal unfinished business. They may waste time trying to prove a point or may concentrate on the clients' history, in order to avoid their own troublesome or unhealed issues.

In any case, this behavior robs the client of time and energy, destroying or at least delaying, the opportunity to work on the issue that's currently ''up.''

GENUINENESS

This is the quality in which we are freely ourselves. It allows for no phoniness, role playing, or defensiveness. Our outer words and behavior match our inner feelings, since we have little need to filter or artificially please the client.

THE SCENARIO

ROSE: [Who has lost custody of her son in a nasty dispute.] While fighting back tears, ''I'm just not going to think about it anymore . . . losing the kid and all. . . . It's just useless to think about it! Oh, how could I have let this happen? I can't take it. . . . I just can't!''

SISTER: Moving closer, touches Rose on the arm, obviously deeply moved. ''I'm feeling very sad too about what has happened, and seeing your deep, deep pain. I feel it too.''

ROSE: Breaks down crying.

SISTER: Quietly shares the moment, responding non-verbally, like a nurturing parent.

THE PROCESS

Ignoring Rose's pretended toughness, the sister responds with genuine feelings. This keeps Rose in touch with the situation on a feeling level, which is also genuine. Bringing the real problem to the surface serves as a small step toward the completion of a painful unfinished issue, whether it is grief, anger, or some other kind of emotional pain that needs to be processed.

Denying unexpressed pain by trying to hold it in requires a tremendous amount of psychic and physical energy. This denial might be apparent through clenched fists or gnashed teeth, and result in headaches or sleeplessness. And denial can lead to making wrong decisions that take one's life off course.

As long as energy is being used in this way, it is not free to flow toward the solving of everyday problems, let alone the most serious ones. Only by facing a problem, and going all the way through the honest feelings that accompany it, can we overcome its grip on us. Genuineness assists by not permitting denial.

THE OPPOSITE

Here are some examples of people who act *without* genuineness:

1) A listener who believes in staying physically apart from the one in pain, possibly even refusing eye contact. This style promotes a distancing approach, rather than one based on emotional warmth. It focuses away from the real issue, the whole family's pain, which can be alleviated only by being expressed.

2) A father who reacts negatively to a son or daughter's situation because it becomes a moral issue he feels compelled to lecture about. Although it isn't easy, the father should own this difficulty, explaining that this particular behavior pattern brings up issues for him and therefore hinders his ability to be helpful, *but that it is not a reflection on the child*. This allows an open discussion to work out the feelings on both sides.

   Therapists might fall into a similar trap, if they are prone to resisting a certain personality type, and let this get in the way of helping. In such a situation, simple honesty is the best strategy.

RESPECT

Showing respect means communicating to others a sincere belief that everyone has the inherent strength and capacity to "make it" in life, and that no one deserves this more or less than anyone else. Behind the quality of respect is the belief that all human beings are equal, with equal rights about choosing their own destinies.

THE SCENARIO

CLIENT (BILL): "I just want to divorce my wife and get busy forgetting about the whole mess! But I can't do it. I really need to stay in there and take care of her, but I can't do that either. Whew! The whole thing's got me trapped. What do you think I ought to do, divorce her?"

COUNSELOR: Concerned, "Gosh, Bill, I can tell you're torn in two on this. Sounds as if one part of you wants to stay, but another part wants to get out for good."

BILL: "Yeah. That's sure it, all right."

COUNSELOR: "Well, let's just talk for a while about that part of you who wants to get out. How do you feel about this?"

BILL: "It feels like . . ."

COUNSELOR: "Just a minute, Bill. This will work better if you stay closer to your experience. Tell me again—how do *you* feel? Tell me about *you*."

BILL: "Okay. *I* feel trapped. *I* want out."

COUNSELOR: "Good. Now go on. *Really feel it, Bill*. It's okay to want out."

BILL: Getting agitated, "I feel trapped! I *feel trapped!* I want out, *really out!*" Then shouting, "*Away from the whole mess!*" Puts head down in his hands.

COUNSELOR: Remains quiet for quite a while, allowing the client to absorb his experience. Softly, "Now, Bill, what about that other side of you, the side that needs to stay? Can you tell me how you feel about that?"

THE PROCESS

The counselor doesn't give an opinion as to the solution, even when the client asks for one, as Bill did in this scenario. Nor is it appropriate to "buy into" a client's perceived helplessness. Instead, the therapist points out that Bill seems to have two conflicting feelings at the same time.

By asking Bill to speak from his feelings rather than talking about "it," the counselor enables him to stay close to his real feelings, and take responsibility for them. By fully experiencing both feelings, the client begins to clarify the conflict, establishing which side is an accurate desire and which is a "should do."

One choice may reflect the person's ego-oriented decision, while the other reflects a deep inner truth. A respectful therapist guides clients, so that they can see both sides more clearly, and ultimately reach their own conclusions as to appropriate action.

THE OPPOSITE

Here are some examples of people who are *not* showing respect:

1) A counselor who tries to solve the problem, suggesting corrective actions instead of letting the client deal with the various possibilities. This takes the power of authority away from clients, whose right it is to decide for themselves. In fact, it tends to increase the clients' sense of insecurity, believing that they're dependent on someone else's opinion.

2) A listener who glosses over two distinctly different potential courses of action, not respecting a friend's honest confusion. Instead, the listener might preach about a perceived morally right choice. Again, such a response would be taking on the role of ''outside expert,'' rather than helping the friend to work through the problem.

3) A counselor who can't take a client's beliefs seriously; for example, professional ethics, religion, or metaphysical experiences. Many people-helpers have the most difficulty with topics that contradict their own beliefs. But they should always be open to what's being said and show genuine interest, even with unfamiliar material.

SELF-DISCLOSURE

This is the act of sharing our own feelings, attitudes, and experiences with someone, in an effort to help the one in need. To be therapeutic, self-disclosure must be pertinent in both content and context. It should be used only with discretion, careful timing, and a good sense of how the information will be helpful.

Self-disclosure can be used at the beginning of the therapeutic relationship to "break the ice." It should never come from a counselor's need to confess or vent feelings.

THE SCENARIO

CLIENT (JOE):   Crying, "I just can't let my wife see me like this. She would think I'm a stupid weakling."

COUNSELOR: Moves closer, showing tenderness. "I know how you feel, Joe. I have a lot of trouble letting my wife see me when I'm hurting. When I do, I feel weak and stupid too. All my life I've been told that men are supposed to be strong, and don't cry, haven't you?"

JOE: Still crying, silently nods.

COUNSELOR: "I'm trying to learn to share this scared side of me with Susan. And you know, it's amazing that when I do, she really seems to understand. In fact, we always feel a lot closer afterward.

JOE: Looks up. With mild surprise in his voice, "You mean *you* really feel like this sometimes too?"

THE PROCESS

The counselor helps Joe feel normal, by discovering that they're not so different, that even professional therapists have similar problems. Self-disclosure removes the uncomfortable sense of inequality, with one person viewed as having answers that the other couldn't learn for himself.

By breeding trust, self-disclosure moves the helping relationship to deeper levels more quickly. When a compassionate listener is willing to share something of himself with the one in pain, the sharer is more free to relax and not be ashamed of issues previously thought to be signs of weakness, or otherwise unacceptable.

THE OPPOSITE

A listener who cannot share anything personal for fear of losing an artificial "superior" status creates a climate of caution and superficiality. In the above scenario, such a person would be judging Joe for getting into some kind of predicament with his wife, or discounting the issue as not being important. This blocks the therapeutic effect of disclosing one's fears and worries. People basically don't need advice; they need to feel heard.

WARMTH

This quality is manifested mainly through non-verbal communication with the person seeking help. Smiling, appropriate touching, and showing other natural responses to the humanness of the one in pain are evidence of warmth in action. Sometimes even shedding tears with a client is the natural human response, and can be very therapeutic.

Counselors who are naturally somewhat cool and detached cannot "fake" a warm response, however; for this would violate the principle of genuineness. These helpers should relax and just be themselves. And they can be comforted by the fact that our capacity for warmth increases as we open more to our own healing processes.

THE SCENARIO

CLIENT: Crying and rocking back and forth, holding her hands tensely in her lap, "Ever since John died, I've felt so lost and . . . and untouched. Sometimes it's just unbearable. I'd just die to be touched. . . ."

COUNSELOR: Leans forward and takes the client's hands. As she does so, the client falls into her arms. In silence, the counselor continues just "being there," rocking, and stroking the client's hair.

The Process

Unlike conventional approaches, the counselor models an ability to be open and responsive, to be human! In this scenario, the counselor acts on an observation that the client had been trying to nurture herself with a rocking motion, and so takes over the nurturing role, as a mother might. This genuine nurturing response to another person feels clear and safe because it carries no ambiguous sexual overtones.

Maintaining silence allows the client to be in her feelings without having to think about responding to comments. Healing occurs as the client stays with her loneliness and need, and feels them honestly. For only by feeling pain all the way through can we dissolve it.

Further, the counselor's responding to the client's desire for nurturing teaches the client that others may also respond to her needs. This gives a subtle, non-verbal message of hope.

The Opposite

Here are some examples of people reacting *without* warmth:

1) A counselor who insists on *talking about* the client's loneliness rather than getting into the feeling state. Intellectualizing might produce some insight, but will do nothing to help the client to actually move through the grief process in a natural and healing way.

2) A counselor who tries to steer the client away from deep pain by discounting the extent of it. Attempts

at cheering up the client with compliments or shallow words of happier times ahead fall short of dealing with the real issue, the grief work that's required for healing.

3) A counselor who freezes under the stress of a human situation he or she is emotionally unable to deal with. Whatever is said appears awkward or irrelevant, shutting down the client and preventing the session's satisfactory conclusion.

Special Note about Professionalism: In order to maintain the objectivity necessary for effective and ethical psychotherapy, physical contact must be limited, and any opportunity for romance strictly avoided. If sexual or romantic feelings should arise between a counselor and client, they should be worked through without inappropriate acting-out.

This *does not* mean that a counselor should not express honest positive thoughts. It can be very healing for someone who has low self-esteem to hear that he or she is beautiful, desirable or lovable—as long as the therapist is careful to keep any such statement from being taken as a "come-on."

Natural, heartfelt warmth is not seductive, and is not misinterpreted as such. The *feeling tone* of therapeutic warmth is different from that of sexual or seductive advances, which are extremely inappropriate to the counseling environment.

Qualities That Challenge

These qualities were also found in high-functioning therapists. They are actually more like methods, however—ways of approaching therapeutic interactions, rather than personal traits inside us.

Using these methods gives the new breed of people-helpers a way of challenging others to be more truthful and real in a therapeutic way; that is, honest, direct, and specific in their self-explorations. Though these traits are seen more often in the professional-helper relationship, they apply in friendships and family dialogs as well. And in all cases, they can be very beneficial to the one reaching out. The three "challenging" qualities are *immediacy, concreteness,* and *confrontation.*

IMMEDIACY

This is how high-functioning therapists keep clients "in the here and now," working on what's truly relevant, rather than running off track, avoiding the real issue. Here the client/counselor relationship itself becomes *the therapeutic tool at work.* Immediacy moves the emphasis away from details of the client's problem (which happened somewhere else) and emphasizes the process *currently underway between the two people present.*

Like a laboratory experiment, immediacy makes use of the "resources" at hand. It connects the actions and feelings exchanged between the sharer and the listener right in the room to real life difficulties outside that tend to keep us stuck. Immediacy teaches clients and therapists alike how to give and receive—expressing and hearing honest emotions (such as anger and affection)—in a healthy way.

This is one of the most risk-taking therapeutic methods because it brings truth right up to the surface, with nothing for either party to hide behind. But it is also a powerful tool.

The counselor or other empathic listener is usually the one to initiate immediacy, and must be prepared for a certain amount of heightened anxiety as a result. Immediacy has two facets: when feelings are positive, and when feelings are negative.

THE "POSITIVE" SCENARIO

CLIENT (NANCY): "I've brought you a little present today. It's not much, but it's something I want to give you."

COUNSELOR: Deeply moved, "Thank you, Nancy. I'm very touched. I'm feeling very strongly right now that you do care a lot about me. Is that what you're feeling?"

NANCY: Blushing and smiling self-consciously, "Uh-huh."

COUNSELOR: Grinning broadly, "Well, I do feel good hearing that! I care very deeply for you too, Nancy. In fact, I think you're a neat lady, you know it? I *really* like you!"

NANCY: Embarrassed, but obviously very pleased,

"Well, golly . . . you're saying that. . . . Well, you're saying that. . . . You *really mean* that? I don't know when I've . . . " Suddenly begins to weep.

COUNSELOR: Allows client to assimilate this intimate moment, by quietly sitting with her as she continues in her feelings. When she becomes more calm, "You seem so moved by this, Nancy. I guess you're really lacking good friends right now, huh?"

NANCY: "Yes, I think I am. I don't know *when* I've felt close to anyone." Weeping again, "And I really want to." Puts her head down.

COUNSELOR: Gently, "Well, tell me something. Are you feeling close to me now?"

NANCY: "Well, yes. . . . But . . . Well, it's scary . . . to feel so close, you know? It's really scary."

COUNSELOR: Very softly, "Just stay with this feeling of being scared, Nancy. Go on into it more. Let it come on through."

THE PROCESS

In this scenario, by dealing with the immediate

process (their sincere caring for each other), the counselor keeps the client close to her reality. Picking up on Nancy's gift as an *indirect* expression of caring, the counselor's own honest sharing enables Nancy to express herself in a more direct manner. This makes great practice for a skill she needs to develop in order to have deeper, more meaningful friendships.

Mutually facing reality on the feeling level moves both parties into a productive interchange. It allows the one reaching out to experience genuine caring and the intimacy of shared feelings, in a safe environment. This provides a corrective emotional experience, counteracting all the times past when it was not safe to express feelings of intimacy.

In addition, this genuine human interaction invites Nancy to look honestly at a crucial question in her life: What can she do to develop closer relationships, and how is she blocking herself from fulfilling this vital need?

THE "NEGATIVE" SCENARIO

WILLIAM: "I'm beginning to feel uncomfortable here. I'm sensing that you're very angry with me and don't want to talk about it. Tell me the truth: Are you mad at me?"

COLLEAGUE: "Well, not exactly, but. . . . Well, I *do* feel like you're not listening to me today. It seems as if your mind is on something else, or you're not interested in me."

WILLIAM: After pausing for a reality check with himself about this comment, "You know, you're absolutely right. I can see why you're getting upset with me. I really *am* distracted. In fact . . . yeah, in fact I'm annoyed with you for not showing up yesterday, and I'm really not wanting to deal with my *own* feelings. Yes, I'm getting clearer about it now. *I'm* really annoyed at *you*. I think we'd better deal with this first."

THE PROCESS

This is an example of a business associate proving to be a real person who, like anyone else, isn't always clear about personal feelings. In this scenario, William isn't aware that he's projecting his own anger onto his associate, until he is asked about it.

But he is *aware* that the meeting was getting nowhere, and that the energy between the two of them had become blocked, as it does when untruth prevails. By bringing immediacy into play, real issues beneath the surface can be explored, with truthfulness leading the way back to the business at hand.

THE OPPOSITE

Using the same scenarios, here are the outcomes of the listeners' *not* reacting with immediacy:
1) In the case of Nancy's gift, if the counselor had simply thanked her and moved on to another topic,

Nancy would not have experienced the direct intimate sharing that proved to be so healing.

Nor would she have been awakened to the underlying issue, that her indirect methods of showing affection are not satisfying her relationship needs. The gift-giving pattern would have been reinforced, instead of providing a new lesson.

2) In the anger situation, William could have more easily ignored the feelings of hostility from within himself and from his colleague. This might have felt safer to both of them; that is, William remaining cool, and his associate not having to face the potential rejection of verbalizing his feeling that he wasn't being heard.

Instead of resulting in a mutually successful meeting, this scenario would have turned out quite differently: a defensive William denying his own annoyance and consequently blocking the truth between the two people, which would result in an unproductive strain on both of them, and a breakdown in their relationship.

CONCRETENESS

This is the act of keeping communications specific; that is, focusing on the whats, whens, wheres, whys, and hows of present concerns. This means refraining from generalizations, ''beating around the bush,'' or abstract discussions. Being careful not to go off on tangents, concreteness invites the ones seeking help to continue talking about themselves and their feelings.

Concreteness also means detecting when the other person is trying to avoid reality, gently pointing out the avoidance, and returning the focus to relevant issues.

The "Generalizing" Scenario

CLIENT (ELLIE):   "The fight with my husband? Oh well, you know, all husbands and wives have these problems."

COUNSELOR: "Ellie, I'm not interested right now in *all* husbands and wives. I'm very much interested in *you* and what you started to say a while ago . . . something about a fight with Pete. Tell me more about what happened."

The Process

The counselor pulls Ellie back into her own experience, rather than helping her to avoid the unpleasant feelings about a situation at home. While generalizing is easier, it does nothing to work through the real issue at hand.

The "Gossiping" Scenario

CLIENT (MIKE):   "Marge is always telling me what to do. It's like she has to be in the driver's seat all the time! Just like last night. She felt hurt, and got mad at me becuase she was want-

ing *something* from me. . . . I never did
quite understand. I just can't figure her
out. She . . .''

COUNSELOR: "Mike, I'm getting lost in Marge and find
myself trying to psych *her* out. Where are
you in all this? What are *you* feeling while
Marge is trying to control you? You look
angry as you're talking about last night."

MIKE: "Angry? No, not at Marge. She's really
okay. She takes care of everything, like
I've told you."

COUNSELOR: "Yes, but you are scowling. And pound-
ing your fist on your chair. I'm not con-
vinced."

MIKE: Pauses, somewhat confused. Begins
clenching his fist again.

COUNSELOR: Mirroring the clenched fist gesture, "Mike,
what's this?"

MIKE: Begins hitting the palm of his hand with
his fist. "I *hate* it! I *can't stand* her always
telling me what to do. I want to tell her
to . . . to go to hell! Yeah, get off my back,
Marge! I'm as good as you are any day.
Any day, *you hear me?*" As anger subsides,
puts his head in his hands and begins
breathing deeply.

COUNSELOR: "How are you feeling now, Mike?"

MIKE: "Better." Smiling, "Yes, much, *much* better."

THE PROCESS

The counselor draws Mike into the issue of his anger, which is much more specific and useful than speculating about his wife's actions. Since we don't have the power to change others anyway, gossiping about them accomplishes nothing except to avoid working on ourselves.

Instead of ignoring the obvious anger, the counselor encourages Mike to get into his feelings, thereby clarifying them.

Expressing anger releases a lot of stored up psychic energy, making it available for more productive uses. And perhaps most important, by giving permission to show his feelings, the counselor lets Mike know that anger is a natural, acceptable emotion. Venting feelings in a safe setting brings instant release.

THE OPPOSITE

Using the first scenario, a counselor who is *not* using concreteness would not challenge Ellie's off-hand comment about fights between husbands and wives. He might even contribute some generalizations of his own, and they could wind up superficially discussing world problems instead of the relevant issue.

While on the surface this may seem supportive, it

would not help Ellie deal with her very personal situation, the relationship with *her own* husband. An agreeable response does her no service. And worse, it also could leave the session in the client's control, resulting in the counselor's frustration, and a waste of the client's valuable time.

Special Note about Avoidance: Sometimes even repeated attempts at concreteness do not succeed. If a client or friend consistently avoids a difficult issue, it may need to be avoided; that is, when someone isn't ready to face a particular painful area, this should be respected. Still, the helper should present ongoing opportunities, so that the one reaching out can continue to *consciously choose* to avoid the issue as long as necessary, and deal with it when the time is right.

CONFRONTATION

In its *helpful therapeutic sense*, this technique is used to bring people face-to-face with reality when an untruth is obvious or a denial is perceived. This can be very difficult to do with friends, and can easily become abusive with family members. It's often better for people to see a professional helper when life issues require serious confrontation. Therefore, the examples below use client-counselor situations. We can all learn from these dialogs, however, regardless of our roles.

Confrontation can be effective when a discrepancy is observed between . . .

a)   what a client is saying *now* and what the same person said *earlier,*

b) what the client is *saying* and what the same person is apparently *feeling*, and

c) what the client *is saying now* and how the same person *acts in everyday life*.

Although confrontation is often thought of in negative terms, therapeutic confrontation is quite the opposite. It serves to steer people away from denial states, which hinder healing, by establishing direct contact with their experiences and creating true growth situations from them.

This is a sensitive technique, however, and it requires careful attention, especially self-exploration on the part of the therapist. The counselor must always be clear about the particular situation and his or her own feelings about the client. This must never be used to satisfy a counselor's need to vent anger or confusion. If a trusting rapport has not yet been established, it is best to postpone any confrontation. A cardinal rule in therapeutic relating sums it up: *Trust must always precede challenge*.

Following are examples of situations that lend themselves to the confrontation approach. In each case, the counselor acts to correct the discrepancy.

The "Experiential" Scenario

CLIENT (SUE):   Slightly intoxicated, with whiskey on her breath, "I'm feeling *awfully good* today! I'm *not even worried anymore* about controlling my drinking. In fact, I'm . . ."

COUNSELOR: "Wait a minute, Sue. I'm feeling very uncomfortable. I'm thinking you had to drink today to boost yourself up just to see me!"

SUE: "Oh, now, wait a minute . . ."

COUNSELOR: [Combining confrontation and immediacy], "No, Sue. Right now you remind me of a scared little girl, feeling miserable, and *worried to death* about your drinking. I don't believe you're feeling good at all. Come on now, what's going on here, right now, with us?"

THE "STRENGTH" SCENARIO (pretended weakness)

CLIENT (TOM):   Drooping in chair, "I just don't know how to go about getting another job. I guess I'm just . . ."

COUNSELOR: "Now, Tom, I don't buy that. Just last week you outlined very clearly four or five ways you have successfully changed jobs in the past, and always toward a promotion!" Mirroring client's slumped pitiful posture and expression, "So what is this?"

THE "WEAKNESS" SCENARIO (pretended strength)

CLIENT (ROB):   "Well, let me tell you. She just can't get to *me* anymore with all that cryin' and yellin'. When she starts up, I just tell her to knock it off right then and there!"

COUNSELOR: Gently, "Rob, I'm sorry, but I don't believe you. You look 'gotten to' even now as you talk about it. Your eyes are sad, you're fidgeting in your chair." Leaning forward, "I believe this problem with Kathy is still upsetting you very much."

THE "ACTION" SCENARIO

CLIENT (DON): "Hi there. Sorry I'm late."

COUNSELOR: "Don, I'm not going to keep my appointment with you today, and I believe you already know why."

DON: "Well I . . ."

COUNSELOR: "You and I both know this is the third time you've been a half-hour late to see me. I'm disappointed and annoyed, because I really like working with you. So—call me when you decide you really want more sessions."

DON: "Aw, come on. Give me another chance."

COUNSELOR: "Nope." Rising, "It wouldn't do either of us any good. I'll see you in a few weeks, *if* you decide you want to commit to your therapy work. That's your part. It's up to you."

THE "IMAGININGS" SCENARIO

CLIENT (PHIL):   "When I walk into that classroom everybody in the whole room looks up at me with disgust."

COUNSELOR: "Everybody in the room?"

PHIL: "Yeah, every one of 'em."

COUNSELOR: "That's hard for me to believe, Phil. I've never known a whole group of people who could all be having the same feeling at the same time, especially about any one person! I doubt they've all even noticed you, to tell the truth. Aren't those people almost total strangers?"

PHIL: "Yeah, but it sure seems that none of them like me."

COUNSELOR: "Phil, what could be going on with *you* that makes you feel so bad when you walk in there? How far back does this feeling go?"

THE "MISINFORMATION" SCENARIO

CLIENT (CARRIE):   "I can't tell my husband I'm thinking about leaving him. I just can't."

COUNSELOR: "Just a minute, Carrie. You mean that you *won't*. There are only three or four things in life you can't do, like going without food.

Now start over and say 'I *won't* tell my husband. I'm *choosing* not to.' Now go on."

CARRIE: "Okay, damn it! I *won't* tell my husband, and I *won't* stop seeing my new lover! I won't! I just won't!" Breaks into tears.

COUNSELOR: Sits silently while client assimilates this experience. Then gently, "How are you feeling now, Carrie?"

CARRIE: "I feel stupid! It's like I do this to myself." Sobbing, "I do it over and over again."

COUNSELOR: "Did you feel the power in you when you were shouting, 'I won't'? That had a lot of strength in it, and it came from *you*. What do you want to do with all that power? What are you willing to do?"

THE PROCESS

In all of these examples, the counselors enable the clients to experience the various ways they keep themselves away from reality, or avoid responsibility for their choices. Once made aware of this tendency, they can learn to take responsibility for their own behavior, which is empowering and a vital step to leading a functional life.

Because the therapeutic technique of confrontation is such a potent change agent, it takes skill and can easily be misused. The therapist's manner and attitude are crucial.

Therapists and clients alike can invoke this maxim: *Let Reality govern my every thought, and Truth be the heart of my life!* This provides a foundation on which to work all therapeutic processes.

The counselors in these scenarios are careful to remain caring, to act from informed and genuine concern for the clients and not from any unresolved issues of their own. This is how honest, helpful confrontation creates deep and trusting relationships by coming directly from the heart.

THE OPPOSITE

Rather than helpful confrontation, here are some examples of people using *harmful* confrontation:

1) A recovering alcoholic counselor who has not yet forgiven himself for his own drinking years, and—with *too* much intensity, *too* much vested interest—confronts a client who is struggling with a drinking problem.

2) A counselor who is insecure about her professional identity and needs to show off her knowledge. As the voice of authority, she spouts diagnostic labels

and offers inferences and interpretations that are inappropriate. This would be especially harmful to a client who may be taking her every word as fact.

Special Note about Avoidance: Although it is extremely important to avoid confrontation when tempted to use it for the wrong reasons, avoidance itself isn't always right. Fear of rejection, being wrong, or some other uncomfortable outcome should not stop a counselor, friend, or family member from ever using this powerful tool. Such fears should be looked at just as seriously as any improper reasons *for* using confrontation. To be effective, a healer, counselor, or anyone else called on in the helper role must be able to confront when it is appropriate.

Total-Way-of-Being Qualities

Reflecting a counselor's overall manner and attitude, these factors are elements of the individual's underlying nature, rather than training. In fact, these personality characteristics cannot be deliberately taught; only life itself can teach them. The two "total-way-of-being" qualities found in excellent therapists are *potency* and *self-actualization*.

POTENCY

This is the measure of a counselor's charisma or magnetic character, the quality that largely determines whether or not others seek out this person for help. Potent people are in command of themselves; they are dynamic, expressive, and involved. They embrace all of life's experiences, both positive and negative, with a deep sense of reverence for life.

Those who are high in potency have *presence*. A potent therapist has relaxed into living from his or her own truth. These people are not incapacitated by adversity, and are therefore models for effective living. Being in touch with their true "beingness," they invite others to rise in stature and practice being themselves as well. Though we can't train a person to "be potent," we can help bring out potency in others by pointing out their strengths to them.

THE SCENARIO

CLIENT (BEN):	Pacing up and down the room, lost in thought, "I just want to work harder on that job out there because I *know* things should be done differently. I believe I could change a few things for the better, if I could just . . ." Hesitates.
COUNSELOR:	Gets up and starts to walk around the room with her client. "You know, Ben, while you were saying that, I got a feel for the sensitivity, and the *power* you've got in you!" Speaking expressively, "I really *felt* it!"
BEN:	"You *did?* You felt *my* power?" Excitedly, "Well, gosh . . . you know, I really

mean it. I *could* do a lot more out there! I could . . .''

COUNSELOR: ''Go on. You could . . . What?''

THE PROCESS

Because this counselor is truly involved with her client, she intuits his potential ''power bank,'' and spontaneously begins to mirror it. And because she doesn't hold back her expression of involvement, she delivers a strong validation of him as a human being. This enables Ben to feel his own power, and to believe in it, encouraging him to delve into his potential.

In addition, the counselor is modeling how to live with hope and enthusiasm. Coming from her own authentic presence, she is not threatened by the success of others, nor does she take credit for it. Therefore, this counselor would continue to support Ben along the way as he functions more and more from his place of power. She would regularly remind him that each step he makes toward effective living is coming totally from his personal efforts, not anyone else's.

THE OPPOSITE

A counselor who is low in potency is uninvolved and unexpressive. Making very little use of inner power herself, she is unable to facilitate the discovery or releasing of power in a client. In this scenario, Ben may have stumbled through his thoughts about wanting to make changes on the job, but he would have had no validation or encouragement to help inspire him. A missed therapeutic opportunity!

SELF-ACTUALIZATION

This is not merely a tenth quality or method for new-consciousness therapy. The extent to which someone is self-actualizing concerns one's *wholeness*, and directly relates to how involved he or she is in a personal journey of awakening. To be self-actualizing is to reach toward one's fullest potential as a human being.

Encompassing all the other nine characteristics described earlier, self-actualization describes the whole person, in relation to his or her individual growth process. And the process is recognized as "two-way," with counselors learning from clients just as clients learn from them.

A dictionary definition of "actualize" would be *to make actual, to make real*. So at its purest level, "self-actualization" means being true to our real selves; that is, being sure our actions are consistent with our deepest truths. Or in a more practical sense, it is the *ongoing process* of becoming more and more in tune with our inner selves.

Self-actualizing people don't see themselves—or anyone else—as "having arrived"; rather, as being in the process of "becoming." They acknowledge that they are fully human, with both strengths and weaknesses. They don't rely on preconceived ideas or dogma of any kind to determine their lives, but honor their own direct experiences as the truth. This frees them to express themselves honestly. Since they value their own individual truths, they can respect someone else's, and therefore have no reason to criticize others.

Whether they are spirited extraverts or quiet meditators, self-actualizers serve as models for creative living. With a sense of humor and a great capacity for warmth and intimacy, they are so open to living that they can be flexible and spontaneous. All in the name of learning more about themselves and life.

In times of stress, disappointment, and even tragedy, they are seldom immobilized, for they are carried through by an inner strength based on knowledge of the deeper journey. They carry a strong conviction that all life's conditions have meaning and a sacred purpose.

THE SCENARIO

TIM: "I'm seeing Beth on the side now. Janet doesn't know. She'd die! She's telling everybody we're just about to get married. And you know how much our folks are counting on us marrying. But I'll tell you, Beth's making me feel really good about some things. I feel like I *need* her company. At least I find myself going over there a lot . . . sort of like a return of old manhood or something. I don't know. Yeah, that's what it is. She just makes me feel like some kind of man!" Sounding determined, "I *won't* be forced into giving her up just yet! I just won't!"

FRIEND: "Sounds as if you're choosing a course of action that feels right for you at this point. But, Tim, I'm noticing too that this choice doesn't seem all that easy for you to make. Maybe there's a lot of pain in it for you, considering the reaction Janet and all four parents might have if they knew about Beth."

TIM: "It's really just awful. I shouldn't be doing this. But, boy, am I confused."

FRIEND: "What a dilemma, huh, Tim? I've been there myself a time or two—having to choose between what I need for myself and what others I love want from me. It's a tough call, isn't it?"

TIM: "Yeah. Well, I do know I could lose Janet either way I go. I mean if I don't tell her about Beth and she finds out from someone else, or if I do tell her."

FRIEND: "What do you get from your relationship with Janet, Tim? Are you pretty clear on that?"

THE PROCESS

A self-actualizing friend is not concerned with teaching or preaching, but with helping others, when asked, to get to their own rock-bottom truths. Searching and growing himself, this kind of person realizes that life is full of ambiguities, with questions that have no "black or white" answers.

In this scenario, someone else might lecture on morals, wedding engagement commitments, or fulfilling parents' wishes. But this friend accepts Tim as a human being who has to face a difficult decision and its consequences.

He also illustrates the relative equality between them, two ordinary men with similar needs and dilemmas. He helps Tim to "reality test" his decision (to continue seeing Beth) against another very real human being (the listener).

In this way, the listener helps Tim to sort out his vague sense of what he should do. He has to separate those "shoulds" that are imposed by the opinions of others, and those that are in line with his own truth. This guides the person seeking help to a clarification of actions that can lead him to face the decision more directly. And because Tim doesn't feel judged by the other, he is free to deepen into self-exploration, and examine non-defensively *all* his feelings. This is the ultimate gift of true relationship.

• • •

From these first-hand interchanges, you can see the new breed of healers emerging—as those who "live their talk" and just naturally guide others with deep caring and respect for their unfolding selves.

Every one of us has a vulnerable, easy-to-bruise ego self. To say we don't would be a lie. For self-evolvement to occur, we need one another to validate, mirror, and reflect us, to admire us and make us valued parts of our dreams and our lives. To help someone else feel "normal" and cherished, in a loving family or group—in fact, in any relationship—is the crux of the healing process.

To be among those who can serve as guides, by their very way of being, is a sacred honor—an honor bestowed on all who are willing to drop their masks and live face-to-face with others right from the heart.

Wisdom from Nature

The following story from the animal kingdom can help us to remember that we are all better off just being natural.

One day a centipede was walking down the street, minding its own business. A passerby was struck by the awesome grace and beauty of so many legs moving in concert, locomoting the centipede on its way in perfect symmetry. "Wait!" said the stranger excitedly. "How are you doing this wondrous orchestration with all those legs of yours?"

Quite willing to explain its structure and condition, the centipede graciously stopped and began to analyze the process. But before it knew what was happening, it became so tangled up in all its legs that it collapsed in a heap. The stranger watching gasped in disbelief: This creature that had been perfectly functioning with natural coordination was now at the mercy of all the threatening outside conditions, unable to regain its dignity.

This story is provided here as a reminder that intellectual analysis isn't always the best approach to life. Rather than relying on mental processes only, acting on instinct is often what's called for. This means coming from the spontaneity of the heart.

The ten qualities outlined in this chapter are essential for consistently effective psychotherapy, and for productive human interactions on all levels. Even so, they are not meant to be memorized like a classroom assignment, or otherwise struggled over.

The explanation of these qualities provides a thorough set of guidelines for anyone wishing to become more therapeutic in his or her human interactions, professional or otherwise. It is intended for use as a reference when communications in any relationship become troublesome. If you were to dwell too much on *thinking about* your therapeutic "parts," however, like the centipede in the story, you too could get bogged down in technicalities and lose your natural grace. And that's precisely how the old ways of teaching went astray!

We should all realize that it is human nature to sometimes become temporarily out of touch with these important healing qualities. Whenever this happens, we need to recognize them and put them to use. For we still always have them in our hearts. These natural ways of being are our essence, and bringing them to light allows us to serve as therapeutic change agents. But concentrating on trying to develop these traits, *as a studious mental process*, is not the way to get there.

To grow into all these therapeutic qualities is to be willing to travel the inward journey of self-exploration ourselves. As spiritual teacher, Ram Dass, so aptly says, ''Therapy is as high as the therapist.''

The only way to bring out our essence is to heal ourselves, doing the inner work that sees truth as love. When we consciously keep our own personal journeys alive with a commitment to evolve through self-knowledge and compassion, then these qualities fall into place rather effortlessly. Becoming therapeutic means being ourselves. It is our highest human expression.

Contrasting Old and New Perspectives

Taking on the therapeutic qualities that lead the way to natural healing puts a different slant on the way we look at *how* people heal, or become whole. Some of the most basic concepts held to be true in the past have gained a new dimension to coincide with the evolving more creative approach.

This chapter summarizes several major themes, contrasting mainstream and evolutionary perspectives. In the mental health field, these comparisons would be considered the conventional viewpoint on the one hand, and transpersonal or psychospiritual on the other.

Some of these concepts have been discussed earlier. They are included here as refreshers, or to expand on the previous information.

SPIRITUALITY

In the old world view, spirituality was a state to be achieved when we finally become "highly evolved." It was often confused with the concept of religion, and tied to particular biases and opinions based on dogma and orthodoxy. This view saw God as a patriarchal entity outside ourselves, who commanded a fearful respect, punished sinners, and rewarded those who were "good."

We now realize that spirituality is our nature. Belonging to no one culture, sect, or denomination, "spirit" is an *internal moving force,* which we experience as a pulsating energy driving us toward identification with our own inner ideals. According to Jungian psychology, spirit moves us toward simulating our inner *image of God.*

Our spirituality is both a goal and a process: As a *goal,* it always feels as if the future is calling us to higher and more evolved ways of being, and to who we desire to be. As a goal, spirituality never arrives. So a "divine discontent" ceaselessly drives us forward. And this is good; otherwise, we might become passive and rest on our laurels while still immature. As a *process,* our spirituality continually unfolds in the form of inner visions, longings, a strong sense of worship or awe, or dreams of the divine, which often manifest outwardly as signs from a higher intelligence.

In the evolving view, God is becoming understood as both loving and fearsome, characteristics that all humans share as well. Rather than being remote and "outside," spirituality is our nature, with us at all times, needing only to be recognized and uncovered as *who* we really are. This is the quality that allows us to participate in our own reality and our own "God nature," as mirrored reflections of the Divine. We co-create along with God. For in this world, we can learn to be God's expression. As sons and daughters of God, we already *are* spiritual; it's *human* we've not fully learned how to be!

SCHOOLS OF PSYCHOLOGY

In the past, psychology largely stressed the conscious-mind world of personality or ego, and depended on set formulas as the keys to healing. While the new psychologies tend to respect and build on theories that came before, they have significantly expanded the scope. Today our psychologies are having to expand, because human beings are! Spirituality and psychology are merging.

These new *spiritual* schools of psychology are ''psychospiritual'' in nature, inspired by the major transformation of consciousness we're currently in the midst of. Besides exploring the personality, they recognize our spiritual selves by focusing on the inner life and the self-fulfillment that comes from being our whole selves, both human and divine. By honoring the fact that humans are both ego and soul, this new modality legitimatizes both our inner subjective lives and the outer circumstances we find ourselves living in.

This inclusive psychology incorporates any elements of the previous approaches to healing that fit with the truth of our wholeness. It believes in an emergent self who becomes more and more integrated, spontaneous, and content, as we progress toward a return to the remembrance of our divine source.*

PEOPLE-HELPERS

The old views saw counselors as outside experts. They

*Schools of psychology are discussed earlier, under *Psychospiritual Integration*, page 37.

were thought to be "already healed" themselves, and therefore could become invested in telling others how to be, based on their own favorite theories about therapy. The new perspective knows that counselors and clients alike are all undergoing a continual growth process, and that the true helper and authority is always within the one seeking help. So obviously, there can be no outer experts! On a path of *Self*-discovery, only the Self can teach us who and what it is.

Effective therapy is assisting others to get in touch with their own inner healers. Where self-correction was the old way, self-empowerment is the new. This is not a matter of *egoistic* power, though, but an owning of our divine right to be who we are meant to be. Today as we all move beyond ego-dominance, we're discovering that healing ourselves and helping others blend with integrity into one process. Humbling, perhaps, but true.*

SYMPTOMS

In the old view, symptoms of intense emotion were considered negative, "wrongs" that needed to be controlled and repressed through medication, surgery, or other means. In the new view, symptoms are honored as the psyche's natural way of exposing its wounds in order to heal them.

Within safe settings, or "containers," emotional releases are encouraged and even exaggerated, so that the root problems can "come on up and out." Repression is now known to *not* heal; rather, it recycles the troubles over and over until they are fully discovered, worked with, and released. Peo-

*People-Helpers are discussed earlier, under *Healers*, page 36.

ple learn best by accessing and uncovering their rich inner lives, and befriending their unconscious minds—including the blockages and dysfunctional behavior that are causing their symptoms.

THE PAST

Finding the cause of our woes from somewhere in the past has always been the benchmark of good psychotherapy and self-analysis. The new view still honors the past as a provider of context and substance, but it eases us away from getting stuck in the past and our limited identities associated with it.

Accumulated along the way as we overcame life's challenges, the past is now seen as beneficial for carrying out our life's work and true purpose for being. This means that we take on certain conditions in order to thoroughly experience them. Then, having learned "from the inside out," we come to know the particular aspect of human nature through and through. Armed with the wisdom gained from our experiences, our intuition is honed for truly helping others in similar circumstances.The shift has moved away from *reacting* to the past, toward a *proactive* view that allows us to appreciate the lessons and inherent value of our pain. This proactive view puts more focus on the unfolding of our future talents and strengths.

FAMILIES OF ORIGIN

In the models of family work now passing out of the limelight, the biological family was viewed as the ultimate and deepest cause of our problems. This was often the only place we looked for a thorough analysis and complete understanding of our patterns of relating.

Now we know that we are "bigger" than we thought we were, that our true families of origin may be clans that have manifested on this earth (and perhaps even elsewhere?) throughout a very long lineage. These "families" have passed along to us talents, gifts, purpose, karmic predicaments, strengths and weaknesses, and other great patterns that both deter us and encourage our fruition.

While the spiritual psychologies continue to honor our current biological families, they place a stronger emphasis on finding our soul groups. These groups are what some feel are their *true* families—people who passionately share their philosophies of reality, where their deepest desires and life's purpose are revealed. When we once again discover some of these soul brothers and sisters in our midst, our family becomes Humanity, and our identities expand. Something deep within us settles down; we feel that we've come home.

THE WOUNDED CHILD

In the world view that's fading, especially within the addictions recovery field, the wounded child was cherished and sometimes coddled as the one who needed large amounts of attention for healing. There was even a tendency to remain this child, to bring it into the heart and allow it to dominate the personality, crying out its needs.

In the new world view, the wounded child is seen as part of our shadow; that is, an inexperienced self who acts out unconsciously until it is recognized and healed. This is the shadow part most easily forgiven, for its image appears in a child's body, which naturally elicits our nurturing instincts. But it is not given such a primary focus in the individual's healing, for that would promote the tendency to "stick" there in our past, in "victim consciousness."

This wounded child now becomes a sub-personality that needs the heart's love, and points out to us the places where we need to be healed. But this child is not in charge of our lives, nor can it be a causative factor in the decisions we make. The child within is called on now to grow up and take its mantle as a mature, responsible son or daughter of God.

RESISTANCE AND "BEING STUCK"

Previously, counselors would tend to fault clients who couldn't respond to their efforts at therapeutic advice or support. They would often unwittingly accuse the client of some kind of failure; for example, being unwilling to take responsibility, or perhaps being too angry or needy to hear the truth.

In the new trend of helping, resistance and being stuck are honored as having a sacred function. These reactions are seen as "holding patterns" the psyche uses while the inner life catches up with outer demands, or vice versa.

Instead of looking down on resistance and "stuckness," therapists express understanding and compassion for the "wise part within" who knows enough to hesitate and slow down when necessary. Paradoxically, this permissive attitude is self-empowering and often releases the client's block, renewing hope that one can indeed change, and the process flows on through toward growth.

SPIRITUAL EMERGENCE OR EMERGENCY?

As people begin to access their internal processes through today's more psychospiritual methods and approaches, they experience rapid growth. The internal changes can sometimes outrun the healthy ego's ability to integrate the material coming up from the unconscious mind. This can create a "spiritual crisis" or "emergency"* when the person undergoing this growth process has no context for the material surfacing, and no one who can validate the experience as legitimate. Being "wide open," people in this state are vulnerable to suggestion by others. And if they are getting the message that they are sick or "falling apart," that can be exactly what happens.

Undergoing rapid sequences of death/rebirth is the psyche's natural way of clearing itself of old issues and advancing toward greater health and wholeness. But whether this type of experience becomes a "spiritual emergence" or "emergency" depends on the person's having available support and the ability to find an acceptable context for their symptoms.

People need sacred, safe, loving, and non-judgmental places to go to for healing and release of the deeper strata of the human psyche. Otherwise, some of these often dramatic shifts of mood and emotion can look like a severe imbalance or psychosis. And the experience can wind up being misdiagnosed and mistreated.

Conventional mainstream therapies have viewed any form of spiritual or transpersonal material as dangerous, or

---

*The term "spiritual emergency" was coined by John Welwood, during the developmental years of transpersonal psychology.

even psychotic, since patient analysis was restricted to the ego. The soul was considered valid only in a religious context. When this kind of material emerged from the psyche during therapy sessions, the patient was medicated to repress it.

One of the major tasks of the newer therapies is to honor spiritual emergence (and sometimes "emergencies" too when they can be realistically managed) as legitimate awakenings, and to guide people through to the sequence's resolution. Teaching to recognize the differences between a spiritual crisis and a psychosis is beyond the bounds of this book, but good books have been written on this subject.* And a number of transpersonal organizations, including Eupsychia, aid students in this pursuit.

PERSONAL IDENTITY

In the old world view, we claimed our conditions or circumstances as our identities, by using "I am" statements to describe ourselves. Words like "I am a flaming codependent" or "I am a chronically depressed person" seemed to express the truth that must be owned in order to be honest about our lives. Anything short of such a claim was considered denial.

In the new world view, the words "I am" are seen as potent expressions of the Self; and they carry the power of manifestation. "I am" holds the essence of a person, which is divine—the One who is never sick or damaged, and never

*For more information, refer to *Spiritual Emergency* or *Stormy Search for the Self* by Stanislav Grof and Christina Grof.

subject to birth or death. The difficult ills we experience, such as codependency, depression, alcoholism, and poor physical health of all kinds, are seen as conditions we *have*, not as *who we are*.

Unfortunately, the English language often causes the trouble with common expressions such as "I am hungry" and "I am angry." In the Romantic languages, these conditions are stated as "I have hunger" and "I have anger," which are more in tune with cosmic law. We become lost in our conditions when we confuse them with our identities, and this only creates more of what we're trying to heal or be rid of.

So we must avoid saying "I am" to anything except our true essential nature, the Self, because of the way human consciousness works: It grabs onto whatever we claim as our identity, builds a life style that fits it, and then "takes it on," actually *becoming what we have claimed to be*. We must remember that the Self is always greater than its conditions.

EXERCISE: Refining Your Self-Awareness

Stop for a while now, and reflect on this message as it applies to your life. On a piece of paper, note what you are currently saying "I am" to. Consider all your various roles, and how you refer to yourself in each of them.

When you've finished the list, read it over, and rethink your outer-life circumstances. Do they uphold the view of yourself, as you listed "who" you are?

If you want to expand on this exercise, rewrite the original list in a vertical column. Then start a column next to it for revisions.

Beside each "I am" that doesn't reflect the real you, insert a new word to more accurately describe yourself.

This is a good exercise to use whenever you find yourself experiencing inner turmoil without knowing why. Pinning down the "I am" you've been enacting can clarify what's been going on that does not align with your deeper meaning and purpose.

• • •

The comparisons given here between the "old" and "new" demonstrate our world's dualism, the fact of nature that tells us everything has an opposite. Unconscious views of this phenomenon see an either/or judgment in every pair of opposites, implying that one is good, the other bad.

The conscious view, however, thinks of this very "two-ness" as *complementary* rather than conflictual. As a new world view emerges, it indeed seems very different from the one that came before. Since the evolved stance is no longer in the negative and limiting grip of dualism, though, we no longer think of all polarities in terms of "right versus wrong."

So within these contrasting perspectives, "old" has no negative connotations. It merely represents an evolutionary stage whose mission is now complete. When looking at "old" being replaced by "new," we see segments of an ongoing continuum, or cycles flowing naturally from one to the next, the ebb and flow of life. A healthy way to view all this is to visualize the *old* as fading, while the *new* becomes more visible and concrete.

Designing a Psychospiritual Tapestry

People today often express boredom and/or exasperation with the obsessive need to focus on their psychological dysfunctions, or their pasts in general. Sick and tired of being "pathologized" (of being seen as "sick and tired"), they are seeking a more spiritual, forward-moving, and hopeful approach to the healing process.

Many aspects of our modern human services work are primed for psychospiritual integration too. While today's clients seeking psychotherapy are also likely to be committed to various spiritual paths, most recovery programs are seasoned in the workings of psychotherapy. And many mental health programs encourage the spiritual philosophy of the 12-Step "anonymous" self-help programs. So the stage is already set for a psychospiritual approach.

Paradoxically, though, medically based addiction programs still tend to shy away from the word "spiritual," while *claiming to honor* a client's "working the steps." This creates an unfortuante breakdown between theory and practice, and has resulted in widespread inconsistency of treatment philosophies and considerable setbacks for clients.

So viewing clients and their families exclusively through the lens of disease and dysfunction is no longer enough. The new-consciousness approach shifts the focus to programs that help people find their own strengths and inner healers. This way, they leave therapy or treatment believing in themselves. We all need to be confident that the Self is larger than its conditions. And it responds best to a path of heartfelt self-actualizing.

Whether or not we are in people-helping professions where we consult with clients, those of us who choose to do inner work can learn to weave patterns of healing around ourselves. Using our own individual styles, we can tailor the colors and textures from our lives to transform these lives into uniquely rich and rewarding "works of art."

Some Everyday "How To" Guidelines

The reminders discussed next can be used as "how-to" information for bringing us back to center whenever we've slipped away from the truth of the Self. By reviewing these basic guidelines, the tapestry can always be mended, becoming stronger and a little more interesting each time we return to work on it.

DRAWING ON OUR CREATIVE SOUL POWERS

First, we may have to remind ourselves that the imagination is good! Many of us have had our creativity programmed right out of us by unenligtened parents and teachers who mistook our imaginings as a waste of time or even "bad." In fact, the opposite is true!

To image something is to create it. Without the use of our imaginations, we couldn't exist at all! Since everything visible in this created world first began as a possibility in the mind, without our imaginations nothing would ever be thought up or "seen."

The acclaimed Jungian analyst Marie-Louise von Franz wrote: "One of the most wicked destructive forces, psychologically speaking, is unused creative power. . . . If someone has a creative gift and out of laziness, or for some other reason, doesn't use it, the psychic energy turns to sheer poison. That's why we often diagnose neuroses and psychotic diseases as not-lived higher possibilities."

Visions from within lead the way to the desired future. When we cannot imagine a certain thing as a possibility for us, we won't put enough focused energy on it for its manifestation. Whatever we reflect on with intense interest and passion later comes to be, for the first stage of manifestation happens with our imaginative cognition. What we truly desire develops inside the mind often without our realizing it. Then, once this is grasped, our will directs it into its proper manifestation.

We build up thoughts or images from our desires. Then a dream coincides with these visions, or something else in the subjective life spontaneously erupts from the unconscious mind and captures our attention. On some level, we're co-creating the particular scenario, cooperating with it. Yet something greater is also going on, something that is beyond the brain's control. This is where inspirations originate, and this is where synchronicities come in.

A **SYNCHRONICITY** is an event or visible "sign" in the outer world that seems to happen by chance. But it matches an inner vision, dream, or longing, which we've already experienced. These unexpected "coincidental" events provide us with direction. Although we make individual choices, we can learn to welcome them as "cosmic clues." Here is an example of the synchronicity phenomenon:

> Suppose you are struggling with a career decision, having spent a long time in an office position, which has financial stability but little real gratification. Suddenly you are offered a job—at a natural-habitat zoo, something you've always been interested in. But, although drawn to it, you're afraid to leave the security of your familiar corporate desk.
>
> Driving home, you see a billboard along the highway. It isn't new; you just hadn't noticed it before. The ad shows wild animals roaming free. . . . Later, your day's mail includes the regular issue of a nature magazine. The cover shows a baby monkey whose big brown eyes seem to be beckoning. . . .
>
> Coincidence? No, these are hints. Your unconscious is trying to awaken you to the career decision *you already know* to be right.

When we notice messages like this, we can begin following their circuitous trails. New-consciousness healers can help remind us to look at our own lives more through the eyes of synchronicity—to learn to trust in these "chance occurrences" that apparently are not chance at all.

We must be patient and allow time for things to unfold, however. Otherwise, we may stop trusting this magical process, causing us to miss the larger life stream that is forever flowing through the subjective.

How to Draw on Your Creativity. . . . When inspirations come, write them down. They pass through us like dreams, and are lost if not recognized, honored as real and important, and recorded. Inspirations produce the natural "highs" of bliss, moments of spontaneous play, and feelings of awe when in the presence of beauty.

Numinous occurrences are those special events that happen from time to time in either the subjective inner life or the outer life that seem awesomely significant, or spiritual. They take place in dreams and our inner visions and intuitive hunches, or show up as "signs" in the outer world. When this happens, the heart has momentarily cleared, and we are in our natural state.

By recording the feeling that goes with these sacred times, you can anchor it, becoming more and more familiar with the qualities of *recognition* and *deep appreciation*. Accessing these particular qualities is healing in itself! Later on, you'll be able to invoke this soulful state at any time.

HONORING THE SHADOW AS AN UNTAMED "OTHER HALF"

The shadow can be integrated only by our recognition and acceptance of it. We don't want it to simply disintegrate and not give us its gifts, for our shadow is our substance! It's our raw passion and true dynamism, which is the force we use to transform our lives. With no lessons to learn, no hurts, no "dark side," we would have no "oomph" to catapult us to a higher place. Our lives might be light, but they would be *flat*. Remember that this "oomph" is one of the shadow's sacred functions. Without this "dark side," in fact, we could have no light. Light does not exist until it strikes an object. Just as we wouldn't know love without experiencing the lack of love, we wouldn't know the Self without experiencing the not-Self.

As already discussed, another of the shadow's sacred functions is to lead us to wholeness. By not letting us deny either half of any pair of opposites, we can learn to integrate them, becoming ever more grounded, balanced, and strong in the process.

How to Honor Your Untamed Shadow. . . . Get to know your shadow, not trying to tame it, but making it a conscious partner in your life. You can do this by repeating the exercise in Part 2 (page 73) until your shadow becomes a familiar companion.

Striking up a relationship with the shadow gently informs it that it's no longer going to be denied, while also letting it know who's going to be in charge. Then its potency fades away into a more cooperative "companion" energy.

As such, our shadow warns us whenever we're getting over-tired or going into denial about some aspect of a situation that is creating shadow-like alarm, anxiety, or perhaps even downright rage or terror. Catching hold of the imbalance as quickly as possible means that it won't have to act out to get its needs met.

USING DISCIPLINE TO REMEMBER THE WHOLE SELF

Because we are so programmed to live from an outer-focused, egoistic viewpoint, and have even been warned that the inner life is not substantive or real, we must discipline ourselves to remember who we are. Self-remembrance must be practiced often to make this subjective state of consciousness our reality. This can be done ceremonially several times a day.

How to Achieve Self-Remembrance. . . . Just take some time to sit down, go within, crossing your arms over your chest, and relaxing into an appreciation of the Higher Self. This brings His or Her image to mind, where it can be secretly admired. After picturing it for a while, enter into it and become your Higher, most ideal Self. This is the act of *identification.*

Afterwards, you'll feel more "in the body," more potent and alive. You'll walk straighter, and notice that things aren't so much of a bother, until the next time you again forget who you are.

NAMING AND DISIDENTIFYING FROM OUR DYSFUNCTIONAL PARTS

Anytime we make conscious a fragment of ourselves that is acting out some excessive behavior, we can, in the moment, stop and call it out.

How to Face a Fragmented Part of Yourself. . . . Ask it to identify itself. When it appears in your mind, ask its name and when or where it originated. Again, the key is not necessarily to tame this self or attempt to squelch it in any way. But be firm about who's "in the driver's seat," while clearly stating your desire for a relationship with this partial, unintegrated self.

Dialogue can then take place anytime this kind of self shows up. The process can be in writing or speaking directly from within your mind and heart. Whenever a self appears that is fearsome, devil-like, or grotesque, command it to "Take off your mask and show me who you really are!"

Once the mask is removed (and sometimes you'll find more than one), see it for who it is, and ask it to tell you what it truly needs from you. This can be a powerful growth experience. It's a way to move from fragmentation to wholeness.

RECEIVING SYMBOLS FROM THE HIGHER SELF

This is especially effective when doing shadow work. The appropriate symbol can be called out whenever our process becomes too lopsided toward one of our shadowy traits.

How to Relate to Your Higher Self. . . . Because it's the Higher Self you're invoking, imagine it coming in from "above" or "beyond." Use the imagery of looking up at a star and watching the star begin to move forward, coming toward the earth from its cosmic home. As it gets closer, identify it as your Higher Self. See it in all its glory, and take some time to honor it.

Then ask your Higher Self for a symbol of itself, to place in your heart, so you can always remember its presence. Receive the symbol, and see how it feels to have it entering your heart. Then move around *as the symbol* for a while. We become the Higher Self by taking on its qualities. This is so key, it deserves repeating: *We become the Higher Self by taking on its qualities.*

BEFRIENDING THE OBSERVER SELF

Remember that the Observer Self never judges us; it only pokes us and says things like "You are losing your temper and are about to embarrass yourself," or "You are turning toward your office, when you meant to go to the grocery store." It simply points out our unconscious behaviors, to give us opportunities to wake up and get back on track. It has no stake in the outcome, ever.

If a voice in your head is reprimanding you, or shaming you in any manner, know that this is *not* Observer Self; rather, this would be an internal critical authority figure coming from some childhood memory that exaggerates the unhappy effect it had on you. If such a voice should bark at you, go higher, and notice it with your observer consciousness. *Anytime* you are being reactive or judgmental, use Observer to go higher to see the bigger picture.

How to Befriend Your Observer. . . . Make a habit of watching for this character within, and learn to appreciate its role in your awakening process. Get to know the Observer Self to discover its state of consciousness.* It lives in a world of objectivity; that is, as objective as we subjective meaning-makers can ever be!

The Observer Self is more objective than we are as our ordinary selves involved in everyday life. It sees a wider view. Observer helps raise us up out of our slumber, at least for short periods, so we can see where we're headed.

---

*Exercises on the Observer Self are given in Part 2, pages 82 and 101.

GETTING "HOOKED" AND "UNHOOKED"

The point of observer consciousness is to lift us above any uncomfortable situation to gain a clearer perspective. From above, we can watch ourselves in operation as we allow certain processes and people to "hook" us, while other situations seem to just flow on by.

What happens when we feel reactive to something or someone? What did the situation call for? What was it that the other person said or did that caused us to react? When we got hooked, was the feeling familiar? Where in the body did it hit? And how long have we been reacting this way? What is the common element that causes these reactions?

Since we act predictably, this won't be hard to figure out. A complex was activated. Roberto Assagioli, M.D., defines **COMPLEX** as "a conglomeration of psychological elements, which have developed a strong emotional charge." It triggers an unconscious pattern of response stemming from a piece of psychological "unfinished business" that automatically erupts beyond our ego's control anytime something in our outer life stimulates it. So a complex becomes activated when a particular situation or person serves as a reminder of that something from the past, an old hurt or insecurity, or some old way of trying to get what we need. For instance, let's take the problem of a "power complex":

This usually means that we've never been given the parental blessing for being outstanding human beings whom our parents could count on to succeed and to master certain aspects of life. We sense that they still see

us as children needing to be rescued at some point, believing we are unable to do very well on our own.

In such cases, a sense of inferiority has built up inside, so that we really do need to prove to ourselves
(and to others) that we are totally capable. Since we have
so much invested in this need to be "on top of it all,"
we can over-react to authority figures, to criticism, or to
being outdone.

Our strong emotional feeling about having to mind
someone or being criticized or outdone is the nucleus of
the complex. Its associate behaviors are very predictable
whenever this particular stimulus comes up in our lives.

How to Get Unhooked. . . . Dealing with a complex begins
with recognizing the pattern and being willing to change
your reaction. This requires much practice in being extremely conscious and vigilant, to catch that tiny moment
between the stimulus and the reaction. Then, gradually with discipline, a new response can be learned.

It often helps to discuss your over-reactivity with a few
people you can trust not to judge you, for externalizing the
conflict strengthens the intention to overcome it. Habits that
are long-lived are hard to break. Yet the free attention and
light-hearted feelings that result once a complex is broken
open and healed make this kind of inner work extremely
worthwhile. Having our identity trapped in unconscious
complexes limits our freedom terribly.

FORGIVING AND RELEASING OTHERS

Holding on to anger, bitterness, and hatred of people who have hurt us is very hard on us. It takes a lot of energy to keep these negative feelings in place within the psyche. In order to hold on to rage and resentments, we have to shut down other more positive parts of ourselves. It's best to release the old anguish, even though the offender may have been truly brutal, and may never change.

Forgiving never releases an abusive person from his or her own ''karma.'' That is always between the other person and God. Our forgiveness is *for ourselves*. It's a matter of freeing up our own precious energy. As long as old hurts remain unforgiven, those who caused the pain still have power over us.

How to Start the Process of Forgiveness. . . . Even if it doesn't seem totally true at first, tell your inner Self that you want to begin forgiving. Wish for it, intend it, and then make it real. This may mean contacting the other person, so that you can work out whatever it is that needs resolution. Or the same thing might be accomplished by doing the inner work of letting go of an old hurt; that is, without actually involving the other.

Forgiveness does not happen through the intellect; it is not a concept, but an active healing force. This pertains more to the emotional life, and usually requires getting back in touch with the repressed pent-up feelings that are associated with the pain. Once accessed, find a safe setting, and allow the feelings to ''bleed out'' in a manner that does no harm to yourself or anyone else.

The Healthy, Integrated Self

Another way to keep our tapestries intact, as rich and vivid expressions of who we are, is by concentrating on our souls' true needs. Although this approach uses a much more simplified list of reminders, it is by no means a simple process.

The main idea here is to remain conscious as much as possible. Always try to remember that a healthy, integrated Self is *in residence, open-hearted, empowered, free of the past, expressive, filled with life's rapture,* and *aligned with its original purpose.* Following is a little more detail about how to bring out these natural traits of the Self.

IN RESIDENCE: Be present, at home in your body, awake, and willing to enter fully into whatever life brings at every moment, be it pleasant or painful. If, despite our fear, old habits, or other distractions, we can keep open, with gratitude for all that life brings us, we can discover what Life truly is.

As often as you can remember, take a moment during the day to stop! Say to yourself, ''I am aware of . . . (whatever you are noticing in the moment).'' Just pause to *appreciate* it. You might try to do this three times a day for practice. Then later, it can become a way of life.

OPEN-HEARTED: Stand in the midst of the opposites, stretching across the chasm between all that hurts and all that delights, for both pain and joy are true and valid feelings.

This is vulnerability in its highest state, where nothing comes between you and your raw natural feelings.

When our hearts are open and activated, we feel childlike and godlike simultaneously. Learning this state of being heartened and disheartened all at once, continuously willing to feel whatever it is all the way through, allows us to emerge fresh and new again and again.

Why not try this now? See how much tolerance you have for this high-intensity state.

EMPOWERED: Develop a sense of having come into this world for a sacred reason, and gradually come to know this as your reality. Remember that empowerment isn't about egoistic power, but your natural right to be yourself.

Feel yourself standing tall and erect, as a rod that links earth and sky. And say to yourself, ''Nothing is *ever* between God and me! *I am* the link! And I accept that responsibility.''

FREE OF THE PAST: Work with whatever condition is necessary to resolve any state of denial, imbalance, or unfinished psychological business.

When something troubling bubbles up from the past, stay with the feeling and let it be what it is. Remember: *You are bigger than your conditions.*

EXPRESSIVE: Be open to the release of the Soul's superhuman powers in the world. This often requires seeking out relationships and environments that are loving, energetically alive, and filled with sacred purpose.

When you feel the slightest movement toward inspiration, capture it—by writing it, singing it, dancing it, whatever. Practice over and over just being your spontaneous self.

FILLED WITH LIFE'S RAPTURE: Let go of inhibitions, to be fully here on planet Earth as both human and divine. Even ecstasy is acceptable! Notice what elements of life bring you a sense of the rapture of being alive. And allow yourself the freedom of "following your bliss."

ALIGNED WITH YOUR ORIGINAL PURPOSE: Be willing to remember—and focus on—what you came here to do and be, and practice serving humanity with all your brothers and sisters here, living as one Soul.

Influencing
Mainstream Practices

Using Our Own Spheres of Influence

Once our personal processes of healing and transformation have reached a certain stability, it is natural to feel "a call to serve." We might enter into a larger sphere, and our influence might increase. But we move into planetary service by the simple act of "doing our being." Your sphere of influence may be large or small; the "size" of your work is immaterial. What matters is the quality of living you put into every single moment.

At this point, we must remember the critical sequence of events: We do not become enlightened and then commit to "the Work." We *first* commit to the Work of Transformation, and then the Work enlightens us! Rising to the call of transformation trains us to gradually learn to live in surrender to a Higher Power, to follow the mystery of the Life force unfolding through us.

For anyone at this stage, the shift is from thinking that we are living life to knowing that *Life is living us!* And with this awareness comes a deep sense of connectedness and sacred meaning for all our individual experiences.

Much of humanity's dysfunction today has a greater purpose than any one person's individual plight. Mother Earth is struggling with the labor pains of birthing into a whole new dimension, and we are being called to assist as mid-wives, to make the birth as gentle as possible.

But we can be effective only by remembering that "saving the world" is always a two-way process: Healing ourselves and helping others are the same thing. And steady workers for the Whole do not allow their personal issues to seep out and interfere with their greater work. *Before we can save the world, we must first save our psyches who think up the world!*

Healers emerging today are here to serve as bridges between a dying world view and one that is not yet fully developed and integrated into society's routine existence. Consequently, their work is difficult, as they often find that the bridges they're standing on are swaying back and forth in conflictual collisions of negative either/or thinking and polarized behaviors.

The strength of the self-help programs is their feeling of community and heartfelt service to others who are evidencing similar real-life problems. Unfortunately, it's so easy for health-related fields to get get lost in the current human condition's pressing issues such as big business, insurance coverage, quality control, managed care, and the masses of paperwork that go with all of it. As a result, much of today's mainstream psychotherapy and treatment programs have lost their spirit while the "lords of materialism" have unintentionally overwhelmed a path of the heart.

But materialism can never rule a true path of the heart! The heart will find expression, or the program cannot survive. And this is why many overly regulated programs are dying today. We must learn to incorporate principles of good business into healing programs that emphasize a sound and practical spirituality. The polarity between making money from helping others and truly caring for them must be resolved.

EXERCISE: **Concretizing Your Sphere of Influence**

Although the preceding information pertains to the world of professioanl people-helpers, don't lose sight of the rest of humankind. We all have spheres of influence, no matter how small our families, or places of work or worship may be. This exercise is meant for everyone—in fact it just may make you realize your "sphere" is much bigger than you thought!

Before beginning, gather supplies for your favorite medium: journal and pen; sketch pad, paint, pastel chalks, or other art supplies for drawing; clay and water; or a computer.

Take a comfortable position, ready to create. Close your eyes for a minute or two, and allow your breathing to become even and relaxed.

Now think about your personal sphere of influence in the world. Who do you interact with during the course of an average day? You might start with members of your immediate family, or co-workers, bosses, and subordinates. Then move beyond the obvious, considering neighbors, people you see weekly or only occasionally, those you talk with by phone every year or so.

These are all people you influence, in a major or less significant way, every time you share a communication. Any one of them can benefit from your doing your own personal work, from your simply being true to your Self. Even if you already knew your sphere to be rather large, you should be able to add to it, becoming aware of those in "background" roles; they too are learning from you in one way or another.

As your mental picture grows, start depicting your "sphere." Use your imagination so that your composite includes as many people/roles as possible, whether in word lists or groupings, or some other symbolic representation.

Continue your creation at least until you've captured the basics. You might want to return to it later, or start anew, once you see just how extensive your interactions really are.

Besides expanding your awareness, this exercise gives you access to feelings about the individuals who come to mind. It presents a good opportunity to come to terms with difficult relationships, or at a minimum to bring to mind some issues that need your attention. Noting your reactions as you are in the process of creating your collage can be healing in itself. And repeating the exercise at different times may reveal much about your personal evolution.

Psyche as the Key to Our Future

Remember, the psyche is a reflection of our Soul. It includes the entire collective human/spiritual unconscious mind. It must be allowed to bring us its gifts of true healing, which can be found only by withdrawing our obsessive focus on the outer, materialistic life, and going deep within. It's time now that we learn to honor the whole psyche, which is both our conscious and unconscious minds, our inner and outer lives, our bridge between the spiritual and material worlds.

Psyche speaks to us through dreams, meditations, and inner images, in the language of symbol, metaphor, and myth. When we consciously merge the mental constructs of "psyche" and "ego," we have created "the Self," which is the archetypal blueprint of the Human Being.

The Self knows how to bring enthusiasm back into our work and our lives if we give Spirit a chance to make its ways known. And the Self knows how to walk this ordinary earth as a balanced and integrated personality—never claiming to be "special" or "highly evolved"; the Self melds into our ordinary human condition with absolutely no need to stand out. We become "high" by simply being our true selves in all our relations.

The basic tenets of new modes of psychotherapy exemplify a deep respect for our total nature. This of course includes the shadow self, those most disowned and uncivilized parts of us that have been relegated into unconsciousness. Until we can recognize the fact that we are both the shadow and the light, we stay lost in lopsidedness—a state our psyches won't tolerate.

The psyche will always swing us to the denied side and bring us painful lessons until we "get" this. Trying to be positive only and to deny any real feelings we have creates more and more shadow. We need programs that help us come out of this imbalanced stance and work through our shadow issues in safe "containers." To deal with the awesome tasks of facing and integrating all our individual shadows and Humanity's collective Shadow too, the world sorely needs wellness programs that honor the whole being —and workers not afraid to face their own shadows!

Those taking a psychospiritual approach utilize states of consciousness that access the psyche's subjective levels of reality, to connect with our deepest spiritual life. In fact, this aspect of inner work represents its chief gift to the mainstream of addiction treatment and other health-related services. Having been in tune with the more conventional outer-directed problem-solving approaches, the people-helping fields are now opening up to the vast potential of the spiritual psychologies that deepen us into our own Source by accessing psyche's buried treasures.

Some of the inner work methods used in these newer programs are meditation, guided imagery, process hypnosis, dream interpretaion, breathwork, invocation, ceremony and ritual, movement to music, various forms of artwork, and deep bodywork. As our consciousness is expanded by such methods, our whole Self takes part—our body, mind, and heart—and we access the *universal superconscious mind* which we perceive as "the spiritual realms." This often results in spontaneous mystical experiences.

These numinous inner experiences have a profound healing impact upon the psyche because they give us intimate connections with our Source. One moment of being in touch with the Self is worth a hundred therapy sessions!

This kind of rich inner work unfolds the most effectively when done in groups of like-intentioned people. With gentle group support, participants discover that all their experiences, even the hurtful ones, have served a sacred purpose for the unfolding life of Spirit. Our redemption lies in this recognition that all our suffering has worked toward the good of the Whole.

And finally, this new-consciousness approach allows clients to let go of the shame-and-blame habit associated with every single mistake they make. They begin to take responsibility for their own patterns and for where they are in their own awakening processes, with no judgment. Sometimes tears are shed over sadness at one's own ignorance. Or the body may still hold anger or rage that needs to be let out. But all this is viewed as the natural and necessary effects of causes now past and rapidly being forgotten.

Each of us can now focus on establishing a relationship to the greater Self and his or her true mission or purpose in life. Putting emphasis on the present instead of the past reduces the likelihood of projecting our particular difficulties onto others. We learn Self-responsibility, and begin to feel a sense of sacred meaning and purpose in all our affairs.

Building on the Scaffolds

Many people today are consciously clearing pathways into the future, building on their unique personal experiences to guide others in this profound journey to wholeness. But how do they pass on *experiential* knowledge that can't be taught intellectually?

Following the basic psychospiritual principle that the healer is within, these people know that no teacher or therapist has the solution to anyone else's core issues. Truth can never be taught; it can only be *caught* by those open to receiving it. Remember? So what do real helpers do? They set up scaffolds for their clients and fellow seekers to build on. And they show the way by creating structure and safety for others to awaken to themselves.

Because the new spiritual approach depends on individual creativity, it has no interest in producing clones of successful people or systems. While the new ways are less rigid than before, however, Spirit does need a structure to dance around, forms through which to shine Its light. So those of us who are in bridge-building roles simply provide the framework, then step aside to watch others fill in the steel and mortar that solidify their own formats and creativity.

It is wise to keep in mind, though, as mythologist Joseph Campbell reminded us, that the map is not the territory, nor the menu the meal. Though we can create great models of reality, such as the human chakra system,* and ingenious formats for our programs, we must never try to take credit for the work others do that awakens them or feeds their souls. Loving leaders create the "set," and Spirit does the rest. Remember too that one does not need to be a professional therapist to be the "scaffolding" kind of helper. Conscious healers come wrapped in many interesting guises—from grocery clerks, to the woman at the street corner, to the licensed psychoanalyst; it matters not.

The Four Pillars of Service

Service is often thought of in terms of physical activity—

---

*A summary description and chart depicting the human chakra system are given in Appendix 2, page 213.

community projects, charity work, and commendable ideals we commit to and take on enthusiastically. But this is not the whole story. The Principle of Service in this world is upheld by four distinct pillars. And ideally, all four should be kept balanced, for the healthy attitude required of those who truly serve Spirit here. All service is an expression of the Soul, shining through our embodied real selves. And therefore, we must know and be willing to work on ourselves in order to stay true to our unique life's purpose. The four pillars of service are *meditation, study, inner work* and *outer work*.

MEDITATION. To meditate is to make contact with our Higher Power, as it opens the channel for us to receive instructions from our deepest Source. It also stabilizes our physical appetites, our emotional reactivity, and our mental confusions. From within, we build up inner strengths and spiritual stature. Through meditation, we stay aligned with our inner Guidance.

People meditate differently, depending on temperament, training, personal interests, and many other factors. Some people run the fast mile; some spin and whirl; some sit quietly in the lotus position for minutes or hours, silent and unmoving. If you are not yet a meditator, find your way, and then make a commitment to spend at least fifteen minutes a day communing with your inner life.

STUDY. When we study the profound thoughts of others, we learn of our true lineage by noting the writers, artists, and saints who fascinate us. As you use each book's bibliography to find other books that attract you, you can trace them as clues leading back through human history, and you'll feel connected to your specific sources of inspiration and true guidance. By merging your own creativity with the ideas of these honored beings of earlier times, your personal expression comes forth. Literature from throughout the ages can help illuminate us and soothe our lifelong sense of isolation.

As you read, watch videos, or listen to instructive tapes, notice whether or not the knowledge you are receiving makes you feel alive. If it's boring, then it's not the living truth—at least not for you at this time. Anything you learn from outside yourself should be only a validation of a direct experience, inner or outer, that you've already had. Trying to memorize another person's way of being is not a valid approach. So remember this, and don't ever let your study become an empty exercise, for ideas can never nurture us if there's no tilled mental soil within us to help them grow. Canned memorizations are never the way to serve. Others need to feel and see *you*, not someone you're imitating.

INNER WORK. In his book entitled *Inner Work*, Jungian analyst Robert A. Johnson wrote: "Inner work is the effort by which we gain awareness of the deeper layers of consciousness within us and move toward integration of the total self." Our repressed issues and emotions can block our true Service in life. Therefore, it is up to us to find ways to stay clear. When in trouble in our own lives, we must take the responsibility to find a safe "container" to vent our need, to express our pain or rage. Otherwise, we give to those we're attempting to help an impure vessel, and can even cause more contamination in their lives.

Sometimes we can find no safe place to "empty" ourselves or to do our personal work. For this reason, it's imperative that we have a method of expressing whatever is bothering us. Keeping a journal is an excellent way to do this. No one ever has to see your journal but you. And it can serve as a processor for your feelings. Besides, keeping a journal can be just plain fun. It makes one feel so creative.

A good therapist or a self-help group of loving souls is your best course for doing inner work. There you will have mirrored reflections to bounce off your issues, so you won't get caught up in your own story lines and keep cycling in old "stuff." And in the group process, our individual healing serves to help the others present.

When we are not working on ourselves, we can take on others' pain and issues without even realizing it—and come home with *their* headaches instead of our own! For when helping others, we resonate to their issues unless we have cleared these issues in our own lives. For helpers, this is both a powerful skill and a plight: through our willingness to merge with others, we can help them to be healed. But we must be careful to come back "up and out" once we've shown our empathy.

Whenever you start to feel emotionally reactive or needy yourself, and unable to function effectively, do take care of yourself. Connect with your Observer, and go inward to regain an even keel. Meditation calms your emotions and aligns you with your inner Guide. Study gives you potency and correct information for your specific work. And inner work resolves your personal issues.

By doing your own psychospiritual inner work, you'll see how you repeatedly experience the "seasons of change" we all undergo in this life. Sometimes we're in a good place, sometimes not. It's the natural way of things. And you will no longer fear or resist these well-grooved psychic processes and patterns; they'll become familiar turf. Then, as a guide for others, you'll have credibility and be effective at what you're doing, for you'll know the terrain.

OUTER WORK. The outer expression of our service is the ultimate goal of all meditation, study and inner work. For how else can we live in this world as the Soul in human bodies, if we do not help care for our brother and sister souls? No one can tell you which areas you are to serve in, for you know your own sphere of influence best. This book is more to help you raise your consciousness to better serve in any area that suits you. We all feel attracted to different ways of serving, as we're influenced by our personality traits, talents, experience, and interests. In planetary Service, all workers are equal beings. So it matters not whether you tend a simple garden that only a few people visit, or wind up on podiums leading large groups. It's all One in the eyes of our Creator.

All Service to Humanity leads to the good of the whole. But to be our most effective in expressing our life purpose, our foundations must be balanced. We must convey all four elements in as nearly equal proportions as possible. *Meditation*, without enough of the other three pillars, can result in living "out of body," and becoming irrelevant for these troubled times. Obsessive *study* can make us into intellectuals who "live from the neck up," a dry way of being, with little relevancy as well. A too-heavy emphasis on *inner work* can bring up much unintegrated emotional turmoil, which keeps us struggling, unavailable to serve any cause. We become the ones who need to be served! And *outer work* alone can lead to a form of "do-gooder" mentality that makes people uncomfortable, where we use our service as a mask for feeling good about ourselves.

And so you see how important balance is. As you go forward in the world doing your work toward the unfolding of your own essence—which automatically inspires others—keep these four pillars of service in mind. They'll serve you well as the cornerstones for your process.

The Path of Sharing Ourselves

Holding steady while the masses plummet into the natural chaos of rapid and dramatic change is how we can best serve in these current times. And while the four pillars of service help direct us, at its most basic level, serving is simply being ourselves, and modeling this authenticity for others. Our very ''beingness''—our open acceptance of life—reminds those around us that it's okay to die to outworn ways, knowing that life goes on beyond our fears, our disbelief, and even our deepest humiliations.

This sacred work of becoming authentic human beings brings us into right relationship with one another and with our world. So ''doing your Being'' is a spiritual path many find themselves walking today. This path rarely leads us into the cul-de-sacs of hypocrisy or self-pride, and is therefore a path of fulfillment and more peaceful coexistence with our fellow travelers. Our modern world is starving for authenticity!

Once we commit to this path and our intuition begins to flow into a more and more clarified truth, all who happen along the way are affected by our essential nature. And by collapsing the artificial boundary between ''the healed'' and ''the unhealed,'' the therapist/client relationship changes radically. From being one of "expert" and "dependent," it develops into one where two souls committed to awakening are becoming whole together.

Although certain professional boundaries must still remain intact, to ensure that relationships remain therapeutic, some of the fences are coming down. This path of "doing our Being" recognizes the inherent value of both our logic and our intuition, both our masculine and our feminine sides, in order to bring about the balance, integrity, and creativity the task demands of us.

Clearing these new pathways through the professional therapeutic community is not for the weak-hearted, though, for it requires bursting some barriers around "sanctified territory" within the conventional world. Sometimes we have to struggle to keep a firm foothold while the bridge beneath us sways precariously for a while.

Sharing ourselves entails a kind of "spreading the word," or passing on what we've learned experientially, but only with those around us who *seem to be receptive*. With heartfelt intention, we can challenge humanity's outmoded forms anyplace within our spheres of influence in the world. Our attempts should always be loving and light, never forceful or combative. We must avoid stepping into other people's schools of thought where dogma or tradition walls us off from open dialogue and honest questioning. Otherwise, we'd be violating their free will.

Fortifications for Bridge Builders

The points given next can serve as reinforcements to

steady us at these uneasy times. They support an overall goal of sharing the awakened spiritual path with others. We should enact these fortifying attitudes in our individual natural styles, and modify them as necessary to fit our particular environment and those we serve. We should . . .

- Align personal desires with what is good for the whole.
- Be willing to note any resistance, then say "I am willing," and surrender to whatever life brings each moment of every day.
- Gather the seed-harvest from the past and carry along only the truly valuable parts, with a willingness to release all else.
- Balance the tension between conflicting ideals by continually reminding others of the good in *all* seemingly opposing views.
- Think creatively and image an ideal future and life's work, according to our own uniquely inspired dreams and messages from our inner lives.
- Become models of authentic living for a world that is starved for Truth.
- Be willing to live with a light and loving heart, no matter what the cost.

The Mutually Inclusive Way

We can be grateful that from the beginning of time our Higher Power has sung a melody in the depths of our being. Its lyrics carry us to the subjective, numinous inner life, where the ego's dysfunctional ways of thinking can gradually fade into the background as we learn to access our deepest truth.

We're being called now to return to our roots, and to a path of the heart. The Self, when acknowledged as a legitimate union of ego and soul, has the power to bring Spirit back into our ineffective and dying societies and institutions. The integration of our psychological and spiritual nature *in practical and understandable ways* is the next obvious step along our road to the full blossoming of our human nature.

No matter how hard we may try to deny it, our very essence is imbued with spiritual life-giving qualities, and our basic nature is love. The time has come to wake up and catch hold of what we know from our modern findings, and indeed, in our hearts: *We are spiritual beings learning to be human*, not mere egos striving to be spiritual. Standing in the middle of our own picture, we can't always see who we are. Our societies, schools, houses of worship, even our own parents, fail to help us see our true selves. In fact, what's being left out of much of our world today is the Self, our very soul!

As we're shifting into a new Age, this is a culmination time for many of humanity's patterns. Right now, the personal and universal are merging, and *all Humanity* as one Soul must enter into the Great Unknown, learning to simply ''let go and let God,'' as the coming Age dawns.

Serving as a bridge builder, willing to do the required threshold work as we enter a new millennium, can seem pretty overwhelming! Are we prepared for such a responsibility? Surely not, if someone had to do it alone. But here's the good news: Even though we may not yet see widespread expression of open-hearted new-consciousness among our public leaders, the number of such people is increasing fast.

A team of like-minded Souls has been growing inconspicuously within an ever-expanding community of spiritual seekers. Inspired by a mutual love of the journey, they form cooperative networks almost automatically, to encourage each other along the way. *This is a true story*, a present reality on our planet. The following description depicts how it might look:

> All of us together make up a long chain of beings, moving upward toward a very high place. The person just ahead holds out a hand to you, while you hold out a hand to the one just beneath you. This is not a competitive ''over/under'' situation, but one of true cooperative companionship. We meet older sisters, younger brothers along the way.
>
> As you are being lifted by the one in front of you, you are also lifting the one behind. Giving and receiving are in perfect balance. In this way, we are all of equal value. Each person serves a vital role in the journey, toward our collective wholeness. As we each rise to the Call, every one of us becomes a vital link in the Great Chain of Being.

Appendixes

Appendix 1

Creating Sacred Space

Whenever you are planning to conduct a group meeting, you can set the stage for healing by following the steps below. Though this is written for a group, similar preparation is just as appropriate for a single client or even a friend who has called on you for help.

1) Have a table set up in the room for the others to place any special objects they've brought that are sacred to them. This table (or a separate one, depending on space and group size) is also good for wisdom books and oracles for participants to use for reference and reflection.

   The books and other items you set out should represent universal wisdom and many paths; they must not be a programming of any one sect or restricted philosophy.

   Be sure to let participants know ahead of time that this provision is available, so they can take advantage of the comfort and inspiration it offers.

2) Before anyone arrives, meditate for a while, invoking the Spirit of Love, Wisdom, and any specific quality that fits the occasion. Then cleanse the area with

sage, a delicate incense, or an essential oil that represents the quality you wish to be present. Never use anything too strongly perfumed, and be aware of group members, so that you can modify your plan if anyone is allergic to certain scents.

3) When the group enters, gather into a circle, and have everyone "go within" for a few minutes. To create a sense of safety, explain that this is the sacred circle where all your inner work will take place, and that it will be "kept holy" for the time you are together. Also stress the importance of confidentiality, and have the group agree on maintaining it, both during the process and afterwards as well.

4) Unless brought in by group consent, keep outsiders away, so that no one feels threatened.

5) Extend the profoundly therapeutic atmosphere you have created by making sure that all activities in the room are restricted to the qualities of love, truth, and acceptance.

6) Before the group process ends, gather into a circle again. Through guided imagery, take some time to open the circle once more to the outer world in preparation for participants to rejoin their regular lives, while taking with them their new-found wisdom.

• • •

Appendix 2

The Human Chakra System

The word *chakra* means "wheel" in Sanskrit, and is conceptualized as a spinning wheel encircling the human body. When a wheel spins, its outer rim moves the fastest, while motion at the center is slowest. Corresponding to our spiritual/human forms, the outer activity relates to our external material selves, and the innermost is like the quiet stillness at the very center of our being, our Higher Self, the center of consciousness.

Many different cultures, as diverse as the ancient Indian in the East and the Native American in the West, consider chakras to be centers of energy that exist along the body's vertical axis. And blockage of that energy is said to be the cause of all physical ailments. The seven main chakras correspond to seven physical locations, and each is related to a specific gland, a color, and certain emotional issues. (Reference chart is on the next page.)

So we can think of seven energy wheels, each associated with a bodily/feeling function. When energy is constricted somewhere, we suffer the result. For example, the solar plexus is where we experience digestive problems, which symbolically correspond to our aggression, hurt feelings, and assertiveness. When energy is flowing freely, we are not bothered by these conditions.

The Human Chakra System

CHAKRA	PHYSICAL LOCATION	RELATED HUMAN ISSUE	GLAND AFFECTED	ASSOCIATED COLOR
7	Crown (top of head)	Manifesting truth clearly. Being one's self. Beginning anew or God-realization.	Pineal	Violet
6	Third eye (between eyebrows)	Compassion for the world. Aspiration to serve the whole.	Pituitary	Indigo
5	Throat	Individual creative expression. Comprehension of one's part within the whole.	Thyroid	Blue
4	Heart	Giving love, receiving love, and loss of love.	Thymus	Green
3	Solar Plexus	Self-esteem or self-identity.	Pancreas	Yellow
2	Sexual or Sacral Center	Passion. Belongingness. Sexuality, childbirth. The creative urge.	Sex Glands	Orange
1	Base of Spine	Security/safety, survival needs. Being grounded or having a firm foundation.	Adrenal	Red

Meeting Your Higher Self (A Guided Imagery)

This is an alternative to the Higher Self exercises on pages 79 and 182, which were written for you as an individual reader. The following practice is geared more toward groups, or for you to offer a friend or client. Pauses indicate where to remain silent, when leading someone else or others through this process.

In preparation, start playing some wordless background music—something beautiful with a transcendent quality. Also be sure each participant has handy a journal or sheet of paper and a pen or pencil. Have the others settle comfortably, sitting or lying down. Then begin by saying:

Close your eyes and breathe evenly as you relax into a light trance state. Just breathe . . . (Slight pause) *. . . Now in your mind's eye, envision yourself walking along a road leading into your own personal new world. . . . See all around you the evidence of this new life. . . . Take in the details of what's there. . . .* (Long pause)

Now notice that a figure is coming toward you from the future. . . . As it comes closer, you realize this is your own Higher Self. . . . (Pause) *. . . Notice what happens as the two of you meet . . . and then merge into one Being. Hear the voice of your*

Higher Self speaking to you from within your own mind. Give it some time. Just listen . . . (Long pause)

When you feel complete for the present, start becoming aware of the room and your everyday reality. Write down the message you received, allowing the inner images to fade as you come fully back.

This is a good time for group sharing, or for participants to discuss their experiences in pairs. Remind everyone of the importance of trusting their own personal interpretations of any symbols they received, their inner Higher Self dialogs, or anything else that came up during this practice. You may want to offer references on symbolism, but be sure not to impose any outer authority's ideas over what a participant intuitively senses about meaning.

• • •

Appendix 4

For More Information . . . .

As stated in the beginning of this book, the material it
covers is based on real-life experience gained from a combination of working on ourselves and guiding fellow seekers
on their individual evolutionary paths. The working-with-
others part of this experience most often has taken place
within the framework of programs offered by Eupsychia.

Our long-standing regular programs are briefly summa-
rized below.

- **6-day Educational Intensive Workshops** are planned
  around specific themes, such as *The Inner Beloved*,
  Birthing a New Consciousness, Psyche's Treasure House
  (on our personal myths), and *Embracing the Shadow*.
  In addition to the teachings, these weeks include
  psychospiritual group processing, integrative breathwork, mandala drawing, working with symbols, and
  other forms of the curative arts.
- **10-day Personal, Interpersonal and Transpersonal
  Wellness Retreats** focus on loving groupwork in safe
  and sacred community settings, where all are encouraged to access and release old wounds, and
  move forward toward their souls' self-mastery in the

world. These programs are especially helpful to people in or out of the healing professions who are experiencing burnout. With an emphasis on healing, they include a wide variety of psychospiritual therapies such as expressive artwork, movement and dance, psycho-drama, breathwork, mask-making, journal keeping, ceremony, guided imagery, and small-group therapy.

- **3-day Sessions on the Western Mystery Traditions** explore the esoteric wisdom of our ancestors, calling on seekers' intuition to enrich their lives through direct knowledge of the subjective and higher worlds. This is practical work, a living tradition open to all, which excludes no creed or religion. Besides the didactics on topics such as numerology, tarot, sacred geometry, esoteric psychology, and the Christ Path, these programs include guided imagery, music, sacred ritual, and symbolic artwork.

All programs incorporate some form of spiritual journeying set to music, and the healing experience of group sharing. Other events not described here include such things as public seminars, celebration reunions, and specific training as requested. If you are interested in learning more about our work, feel free to call the office, or fill out the enclosed card and mail it to us.

• • •

Eupsychia, Inc. • P.O. Box 3090 • Austin TX 78764
Phone: 512-327-2795 • Fax: 512-327-6043
EMail: eupsychia1@aol.com

Acknowledgments

In Appreciation . . . . .

. . . . for Mary Yovino and her undaunted faith, intentionality and hard work in putting all this material from our workshop experiences and fragments of writing into book form. This project would never have happened without her.

. . . . for Brenda Shea, Eupsychia's steady "Captain of Daily Operations," whose integrity and precision, not to mention her long hours of dedication, keep our doors open and our lines accessible to those who seek us out.

. . . . and to all who journey with us in Eupsychia's "living laboratory" for the experiential study of the self-in-transformation. You are continually my inspiration!

—*Jacquelyn Small*

My acknowledgments have to begin with gratitude for the life circumstances that steered me from an often tedious corporate career into the freelancing that satisfies my soul. . . . Of all the people who have offered encouragement about following my dreams, I especially appreciate longtime colleague and friend Alyce Hanson—for her unwavering support on many levels. . . . I thank our chief guides at DeVorss & Company, Hedda Lark, Arthur Vergara, and Gary Peattie; also Gabriel Molano for his inspired cover illustration. . . . And most of all, I'm grateful for Jacquelyn Small's introduction to spiritual psychology, and so much more. Through compassion, wit, and sometimes uncomfortable challenges, Jacquie has been a major influence on my "evolution" since the day we met.

—*Mary Yovino*

About the Authors

JACQUELYN SMALL, LMSW, is recognized as an inspiring facilitator, therapist and author of several defining books on spiritual psychology and the transformational process. Her books include *Becoming Naturally Therapeutic, Transformers: The Artists of Self-Creation, Awakening in Time* and *Embodying Spirit.* She is widely hailed for her pioneering synthesis of psychology and metaphysics, and serves a bridging function between conventional and transformational psychology and religion. Jacquelyn is a Phi Beta Kappa graduate of the University of Texas with degrees in psychology and clinical social work and has over twenty years' experience conducting workshops and seminars in personal transformation. She is Founding Director of Eupsychia, Inc., an institute for education, training, and healing, which certifies people in spiritual psychology. She lives in Austin, Texas.

MARY YOVINO is a former technical writer/editor and Information Development Manager with a degree from the State University of New York and many years' experience in the business world. Having discovered the curative arts during her own spiritual journey, she became an avid student of Jacquelyn Small's teachings. Now certified in Psychospiritual Integration and as a Breathwork Practitioner, Mary focuses on sharing what she's learned—especially through the written word. Besides an ongoing affiliation with Eupsychia, she serves as editor and as designer of marketing materials for various peers in the Work. From her home in Ft. Lauderdale, Florida, she is currently co-authoring a book on the transformational stories of ordinary people.